Reference Guide
for the
LifeWeaving
Dowsing Charts

POWER, RESEARCH
AND
PRSM CHARTS

CAROLE CONLON, L.Ac.
Master Integrational Healer

AyniWrite Press
Albuquerque, NM

Carole Conlon/AyniWrite Press
Albuquerque, NM
www.AyniWritePress.com

Edited by Barbara J. Rose
Book Layout ©2013 BookDesignTemplates.com

Ordering Information:
For quantity sales: Special discounts are available on quantity purchases by corporations, associations, and others. For details, contact the publisher through AyniWritePress.com.

Reference Guide for the LifeWeaving Dowsing Charts --- Power, Research and PRSM Charts / Carole Conlon. —1st Ed.
ISBN 978-0-9907550-3-6

The Transmuting Violet Flame Prayer

Holy Father/Mother God, Creator of all that is,
I call on the Law of Forgiveness for myself and all mankind
for all mistakes, mis-qualified energy
and for straying from the Light.
Holy Father/Mother God, Creator of all that is,
blaze through me the Limitless Transmuting Violet Flame,
Thy Sacred Fire,
and Transmute now all impure desire, hard feelings,
wrong concepts, imperfect etheric records,
causes, effects and memories, known or unknown,
in this life time or any other lifetime,
in all dimensions of my subtle body
and physical body.
Keep this flame sustained and all powerfully active.
Replace this karma with pure substance,
power of accomplishment and the divine plan fulfilled.
Charge me with perfect health,
joy,
happiness,
illumination,
love,
wisdom,
power
and abundance
in the name of the Cosmic Christ Vibration.

Amen

Contents

Transmuting Violet Flame Prayer iii

Preface xiii

Introduction xv

Section One: POWER CHART

Chapter 1

LifeWeaving and the Power Chart 3

    The LifeWeaving Process Defined 3

    Power LifeWeaving Chart 5

    Basic LifeWeaving Protocol 5

Chapter 2

Power Chart Key, Yes-No & Number Chart 9

    Working with the Chart Key...9

    Working with the Yes-No and Number Charts............................10

Chapter 3

Permission to Work & the *Invocation* 11

    What the Invocation Accomplishes 12

    Using the Worksheet to Check for Preparedness 14

Chapter 4

Power Chart Section A 15

    Directional Ring 15

    Life Areas 16

    Colors 18

    The Elements 19

    Call Upon/Use 21

    Chakras 23

    Activities 24

    Affirmations 25

    Responsible To/For 27

Chapter 5

Power Chart Section B 29

Directional Ring 29

Source of Information/Who is Involved 30

Three Kingdoms 31

Time 33

Body Levels 33

Mayan Consciousness Scale 35

Body Categories 37

Chapter 6

Power Chart Section C: Archetypes 39

Introduction to Archetypes 39

Shadow Aspects of Archetypes 40

Role of Archetypes in Dis-ease and LifeWeaving Clearing 42

Protocol for Testing that Archetypes Have Cleared 43

Using the Archetype Chart Section 43

Archetype Definitions and Energy Pictures 44

Section Two: RESEARCH CHART

Chapter 7

LifeWeaving and the Research Chart 87

Introduction 87

Research Chart Protocol... 88

Chapter 8

Research Chart Section A 91

Yes and No 91

Numbers 92

Directional Ring 92

Dowsing Questions 92

Relationships 95

Time 97

Check Instead 99

The Keyword Petals 101

Chapter 9
Research Chart Section B : Blocks 103
   Introduction to Blocks Seal 103
   Types of Blocks 104

Chapter 10
Research Chart Section C: Blessing Seal 109
   The Blessing Seal 109
   Using the Blessing Seal 110

Chapter 11
Completion Check and Clearing Macro 111
   Clearing Macro 111
   Clearing Macro Protocols 112
   Completion Check 113

Section Three: PRSM DIAGNOSTIC CHART
Disclaimer 116
Chapter 12
Dis-ease, Energy and Medical Dowsing 117
   The Theory of Dis-ease 117
   Medical Dowsing as a Healing Tool 118

Chapter 13
LifeWeaving and the PRSM Chart 123
   PRSM Chart 123
   PRSM Diagnosis Protocol 125
   An Example of Working with PRSM Diagnosis 126

Chapter 14
PRSM Section A: Key and Descriptors 133
   Source of Pendulum Information 133
   PRSM Categories 135
   Numbers and Left-Right 136
   Body Levels /Levels of Dis-ease 136

Descriptors Chart 139

Subcategories, Modifiers and Identifiers 140

Chapter 15

PRSM Section A: Environmental Factors 143

Introduction 143

Environmental Descriptors 144

    Stress 144

    Allergies 144

    Electro-Magnetic 146

    Chemical 146

    Iatrogenic 147

    Nutritional 148

    Radiation 148

    Ley Lines/Toxic Streams 148

    Other (People...Place...Thing) 149

Chapter 16

PRSM Section A: Hormonal Factors 151

Introduction 151

Hormonal Descriptors 152

    Gonads 152

    Adrenals 152

    Liver 153

    Thymus 153

    Parathyroid 153

    Thyroid 154

    Hypothalamus 155

    Pituitary 156

    Other 156

Chapter 17

PRSM Section A: Infection Factors 157

Introduction 157

Infection Descriptors 157

    Toxins 158

    Parasites 158

    Viral 159

Bacterial 159

Yeast/Fungus 160

Stones/Sludge 160

AIDS/ARC 161

Cancer 161

Other 162

Infection Modifiers 162

Chapter 18
PRSM Section A: Internal-Meridial Factors 165

Introduction 165

Internal-Meridial Descriptors 166

Brain 166

EENT (Ears/Eyes/Nose/Throat) 166

Heart 168

Small Intestine 168

Bronchi & Lungs 169

Large Intestine & Appendix 169

Spleen 170

Stomach/Pancreas 171

Liver 172

Gallbladder 172

Kidneys 173

Urinary Bladder 174

Other 174

Endocrine 174

Chapter 19
PRSM Section A: Structural Factors 177

Introduction..177

Structural Descriptors..179

Cranium..179

Atlas..179

Jaw or Temporal Mandibular Joint....................179

Neck..180

Thoracic..180

Arms..180

Hands/Wrists/Elbows/Shoulders........................181

Lumbar 181

Sacrum 181

Feet/Ankles/Knees/Hips 182

Legs 182

Other 182

Structural Identifiers Descriptors 182

Lymph System 183

Bones 183

Diaphragms 184

Muscles/Tendons 184

Scar Tissue 184

Skin/Cells 185

Blood Vessels 185

Other 185

Nerves 185

Chapter 20

PRSM Section A: Emotional Factors 187

Introduction 187

Emotional Descriptors 188

Scars/Blocks 188

Chemical Imbalance 188

Psychic Attack 189

Other 189

Chapter 21

PRSM Section A: Chakras 191

Introduction 191

Chakra Descriptors 191

Alpha 192

Soul 192

Crown 193

Brow 193

Alta Major 194

Throat 195

Thymus 196

Heart 196

Hand 197

Solar Plexus 198

Abdominal 198

Root 199

Foot 200

Omega 200

Working with Chakras 201

Chapter 22

PRSM Section B: Deaths - How and Why 203

Introduction 203

Elements of Section B 204

PRSM Section B Protocols 205

Appendix One: Critical Differences Between

Standard and LifeWeaving Dowsing 207

Harmonize the Personal Trinity - the Self, Soul and Ego 207

Each Dowsing Sequence Begins on a Neutral Line 208

Each Dowsing Sequence Ends on a Neutral Line 208

Allow for Multiple Answers 208

When Dowsing a Section is Completed, Return to the Chart Key
....208

Create an Imaginary Basket to Hold Answers Until Ready to Clear
....209

Recognize that a New Layer is Ready to Clear 209

Test a Variation of the Original Issue 209

Do a Final Completion Check After Clearing 209

Appendix Two: The Worksheet 211

Bibliography 213

Index 217

Meet the Author 235

Preface

The LifeWeaving charts are a result of weaving a long journey of personal studies with many superior and pivotal teachers. Barbara Wallace first introduced me to pendulum work and started me on the path over 40 years ago. Next Robert Detzler presented a new level of work with his Spiritual Response Therapy system of pendulum charts. As I used his dowsing system, I saw the potential of moving away from traditional dowsing and took the liberty to begin creating my own charts and system. Freedom!

Big thanks to former student and good friend Barbara J Rose who has used her editing skills and knowledge of this work to help make my words more understandable. I also have to thank Hoy Ping Yee Chan, one of my acupuncture teachers from years ago and now a friend, who let me help her publish her professional book, *Chinese Medicine for Aging Eyes*, making me knowledgeable and confident enough to publish my own. I also send huge a thank you to all my acupuncture clients who put up with my explorations as I developed the LifeWeaving system, and those that still call for help.

The LifeWeaving clearing system went through many name changes during its development—each time getting a good trial run that resulted in more modifications. Eventually the complete body of knowledge known as LifeWeaving was carefully transferred to three charts and accompanying manuals.

However, a constant voice in my ear demanding more simplification came from friend and former student Brian T Roberts who pressed for clearer instructions and a simpler form for the method. So Brian and I put our heads together to create a chart for beginners—a chart simple enough that self-clearing would be a breeze for anyone to use. Thus the POWER LIFEWEAVING CHART was born.

I began using this new chart on clients and found that issues often cleared without a need for further research. As a result,

POWER LIFEWEAVING is the primary chart I use for clearing myself and others. The answers don't always make sense, the picture of what happened doesn't fill in as when using the three chart system, but POWER LIFEWEAVING clearing has proven itself as an effective step in clearing myself and others.

However, as a chart for beginning dowsers, POWER LIFEWEAVING still proved to be too complicated. Before working with these charts, a dowser should have pendulum skills, know how to work with basic charts, and possess a good dose of common sense.

So a very special thanks to all those helpful earthly friends as well as the master spirits and elementals who continue to guide the process. With their help, I present this "final" installment to the **LifeWeaving** system of clearing.

From the breath of God's Light
I Am, I Am, I Am,
Carole

Gratitude!

Introduction

LifeWeaving has evolved over the past 20 years by developing each dowsing chart in turn, then often revising and reorganizing the information. As the years went by, chart content as well as how they were used also changed to match the ever increasing frequencies enveloping the Earth and those of us on it.

I felt it was important to reorganize the body of work into a concise form as a means of simplifying and sharing the information and techniques with other dowsers and healers who might be interested. Therefore, in the past year, with changes to the three main charts completed, the LifeWeaving method has finally stabilized in this latest form.

The POWER CHART is the heart of the LifeWeaving system, and provides enough information to identify and clear many emotional blocks that have locked up a person's energy fields. The RESEARCH CHART provides the means to identify added details such as relationships, time, energies, types of blocks along with questions to ask if stumped about what to do next. The PRSM CHART, developed first, provides information about the body systems and levels for diagnostic inquiry.

The charts can be used individually or as a set, linked by chart keys to enable more automatic dowsing and an easier flow from one section or chart to another.

In addition to the LifeWeaving information in this *Reference Guide*, I have included additional healing information accumulated over the 28 years of practice as a licensed acupuncturist and energy worker.

More charts are in the works as necessity, interests and change dictate.

This *Reference Guide* to the LifeWeaving charts is meant to be just that - a reference. Feel free to read it cover to cover as an overview of the three charts or look at it when questions about certain chart elements come up during a session. If you are new to LifeWeaving, it is very important to read Appendix One to learn how LifeWeaving dowsing differs from traditional dowsing as well as different ways to test using these charts. I've also included a complete index to make look up easier.

I welcome feedback, constructive criticism and suggestions - especially new ways to use the LifeWeaving charts for healing. And I would love to hear from previous students to see how they have worked with the system and what changes they have made.

As we move further through this ascension process, in a few years this type of work will hopefully be unnecessary. Until that happens, LifeWeaving can be an exceptional tool to help people clear away layers of emotional blocks and cellular memories of past lessons still needing to be released. I'm happy to be sharing the LifeWeaving method with you.

I AM, I AM, I AM

Carole
Albuquerque, NM

LOVE

THE POWER CHART

CHAPTER 1

LifeWeaving and the Power Chart

Figure 1 LifeWeaving Symbol

The LifeWeaving Process Defined

LifeWeaving, a multidimensional dowsing method, uses special charts to help identify and immediately remove emotional blockages that are layered throughout the body. This clearing process is designed to move a person into a state of neutrality, where everything exists without emotional baggage, biases or feelings.

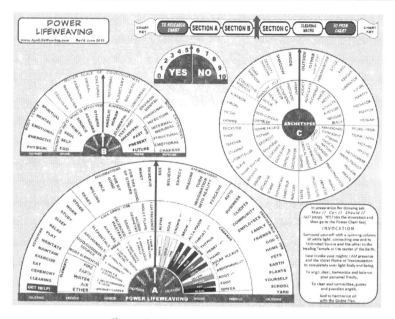

Figure 2 LifeWeaving POWER CHART

LifeWeaving is a tool you can use to seek answers, to nourish and enhance your life, and to empower yourself on a daily basis to meet life's "little challenges." Living life from a neutral point of view can bring great reward and enable you to deal with stress more easily.

The basic LifeWeaving process is simple. By dowsing the charts, a question, situation, relationship or even an illness is translated into a set of word frequencies that match the issue. As the words are dowsed, they are collected together into a "holding basket." Once the *Clearing Macro* is indicated, the contents of the basket are spiraled throughout the body to remove the blocking energy signatures, just as identical sound frequencies, inverted 180 degrees over each other, nullify each other ending in silence. Once these blocks are cleared, the frequency of unconditional love is infused back through the body to complete the healing.

In this manual, the elements of the various chart sections will be presented along with definitions and tips on how to use them.

Power LifeWeaving Chart

POWER LIFEWEAVING is the foundational chart used for the clearing process and can be used either by itself or in conjunction with the other charts in the system. Before beginning a session, set your intention about which charts you intend to use and then ask spirit to give answers within those limits.

Basic LifeWeaving Protocol

Prepare for the Session

1. Prepare to work by clearing yourself and your surroundings.
2. Obtain permission to work on your patient by asking: *"May I?" "Can I?" "Should I?"*
3. Set up a healing grid around your patient and place a White Light tunnel between the two of you.
4. Harmonize with the client's energy.

Invocation to Clear the Client

Say to the client: *"Create a spinning* (either direction) *column of White Light around yourself, connecting one end to Unlimited Source and the other to the Healing Temple at the center of the Earth.*

Now invoke your mighty I AM presence and the Violet Flame of Transmutation to completely over light body and being,

To align, clear, harmonize and balance the Personal Trinity; to clear the soul committee, guides and guardian angels; and to harmonize all with the Divine Plan."

Protocol Steps

1. Use the **LifeWeaving** worksheet to confirm that the *Invocation* clearing was successful by using the *Check List for*

Preparedness questions 1 - 11. Then ask any of the *Supplemental Questions* as needed or desired.

2. Align your pendulum on the POWER *Chart Key* neutral line and, using intention, add in the client and the issue or statement being tested, and ask: "*What is needed to help?*" (or other question of your choice).

3. Follow the dowsed directions to the appropriate chart section and collect (dowse for) any related *Keyword(s),* placing them into a 'holding basket' until your pendulum remains at neutral on the section neutral line.

4. Return to and dowse the POWER *Chart Key* for the next action. Ask "*Anything else?*"

5. Always sending any results to the holding basket, continue testing indicated chart sections until the pendulum points to the *Clearing Macro* on the *Chart Key*.

6. Run the contents of the holding basket through the body, mind and spirit while saying the *Clearing Macro,* found on the RESEARCH CHART.

7. Ask "*Is there anything else contributing to the issue, or that I should ask about instead?*" If "*yes,*" continue testing. *Note:* if your pendulum indicates a new layer at this time, continue testing.

8. Do a *Completion Check,* found on the RESEARCH CHART, for the issue/statement you have just tested and cleared.

   o "*Is this issue clear for the client's ego, self, soul and spirit helpers?*"
   o "*Is the issue clear on all levels?*" "*Physical?*" "*Energetic?*" "*Emotional?*" "*Mental?*" "*Spiritual?*"

9. Take any positive answers from step 8 to the POWER *Chart Key* neutral line and continue testing (Steps 2-8) until your pendulum remains at neutrality for the original statement or question.

10. Continue with your next line of inquiry. (Steps 2-9)

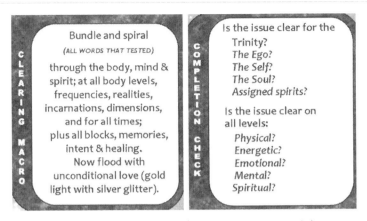

Figure 3 The *Clearing Macro* (L) and *Completion Check* (R)

Complete the Healing

1. Have the client spiral unconditional love (gold light with glitter) through his/her body, mind and spirit. This should usually be done after clearing a particular issue and you feel the process is complete.

2. Do generational clearing by sending all the healing that has occurred during the session seven generations back on both the mother's and father's side.

3. Follow with more unconditional love for both client and ancestors.

Close the Session

1. Give thanks to all spiritual helpers who assisted during the session.

2. Close down the White Light tunnel and disconnect yourself energetically from the client.

3. Suggest that the client renew his/her column of White Light, the Violet Flame and *I AM* presence.

CHAPTER 2

Power Chart Key, Yes-No & Number Chart

Working with the *Chart Key*

Figure 4 POWER *Chart Key*

As you begin dowsing any of the *Chart Keys* or chart sections, train your pendulum to always return to the neutral line and remain there in a neutral swing to show completion. *E.g.,* if you are directed to POWER *Section A, Colors,* your pendulum indicates the *Keywords* white, gold and pink (they go into the "holding basket"); then the pendulum returns to the *Section A* neutral line and remains in a gentle neutral swing. That signals you to return to and dowse the *Chart Key* again for your next action.

If you are only using the **LifeWeaving** POWER CHART, ignore the "To RESEARCH" and "To PRSM" options on the *Chart Key* and instruct your pendulum to only consider the POWER CHART sections during the inquiry.

Figure 5 Yes, No and Number Chart

Working with the Yes-No and Number Chart

Use this chart either where a simple *"yes"* or *"no"* is required or to find percentages and numbers. Because life is seldom all good or all bad, it is best to ask *"What percent good?"* and *"What percent harm?"* The numbers 1-10 become 10-100% for this option.

When testing for a number, first ask *"How many digits are in the number?"* and then ask to see them. For example, the pendulum may first indicate the number of digits is 3; then swings in turn to the 6, the 5 and then the 9. The number is 659. Alternately, if you are searching for a specific number like a four-digit year, you can simply ask to see the number since you already know its size.

CHAPTER 3

Permission to Work and the *Invocation*

The *Invocation* is an essential step to help ensure the quality and completeness of answers in this chart clearing work. Dowsing often fails because of faulty answers coming from poor questions or a suspect information source. This makes the initial clearing and alignment of both the dowser and client extremely important. Use of the *Invocation* is an attempt to secure the best results possible.

Before reading the *Invocation,* obtain permission to work. If you are doing POWER LIFEWEAVING clearing on yourself, as you read the *Invocation,* just change the words (you, your, etc.) to fit (I, me, mine).

In preparation for dowsing ask:
May I? Can I? Should I?
NO? (stop). *YES?* (do the invocation and then go to the Power Chart Key)

INVOCATION
Surround yourself with a spinning column of white light, connecting one end to Unlimited Source and the other to the Healing Temple at the center of the Earth.

Now invoke your mighty *I AM* presence and the Violet Flame of Transmutation to completely over light body and being,

To align, clear, harmonize and balance the personal Trinity,

To clear soul committee, guides and guardian angels,

And to harmonize *all* with the Divine Plan.

Figure 6 Permission and the *Invocation*

Once this initial clearing work is completed, the client will often feel much better - even if his or her presenting complaint has not yet been addressed.

What the *Invocation* Accomplishes

Reading the *Invocation* before a LifeWeaving session performs five important specific functions.

1. **The *Invocation* sets up protection and connects you to Source and the grounding Earth**.

   Dark forces do not like White Light, which contains the energies of all elements and chemicals found in the sun and represents Totality, the Absolute, or the Holy Trinity. Spinning a column of White Light around your body offers protection and causes worldly thoughts and feelings to bounce off. Connecting the column to Source gives you unlimited strength while the connection to the Earth allows continual grounding and an outlet for the energy being cleared.

2. **The invocation invokes your mighty *I AM* presence and the Violet Flame of Transmutation.**

   The *I AM* Presence is the divine spark of Totality in all humans; a sacred connection with one's true self; the Christ within. The Violet Flame transforms unwanted conditions and balances all by its Light.

3. **The *Invocation* harmonizes your *Personal Trinity* - your Ego, Self, and Soul.**

   The term *Personal Trinity* is used to describe the three parts of our functioning organism - the Ego, Self, and Soul. All three parts have a direct effect upon one's life.

   - The **Ego** responds primarily to fears and memories, and mostly affects the three lower chakras in matters of safety concerns for the physical body.

- The **Soul** or **High Self** is concerned with spiritual development and relates more to the three upper chakras.

- The **Self**, which should operate out of the heart chakra, sits between Ego and Soul and receives information to be considered and potentially acted upon during the course of life.

To obtain answers, a dowser typically connects to the High Self of the client. Everyone's High Self (also called the Soul Committee) has the assigned task of determining each person's "highest and best good" and is therefore considered to be the best source for dowsing accuracy. Yet in healing work, we also need to take into account input from our most wounded part, the Ego. The Ego strongly influences the condition of the body, often getting attention by broadcasting signals such as pain or emotions. The dowser also needs to consider that the human Self makes major decisions and has many belief systems that affect its outlook on life. Thus, in order to heal the physical, a dowser must also include the Ego and Self (both aligned with the Soul) in the testing, clearing and decision-making process.

4. **The *Invocation* clears the soul committee, guides and guardian angels.**

    Your High Self Soul Committee acts like a spiritual nanny watching over your spiritual growth. Therefore members of your Soul Committee should be at the highest frequency level (usually archangels, ascended masters, etc.) and this Committee should be small (9 or 11 is optimal). It is also best if the Committee has an uneven number of spirits on board so there is never a "tie vote."

    Once in a while guides and guardian angels need to be cleared, removed or upgraded because we sometimes collect too many, they might be at a lower frequency than we are, or our own needs have changed where we need helpers with different expertise. To upgrade say: "*Educate, elevate, remove and replace.*" You can expand on this basic statement by identifying the type of spirits you want to invite in (*e.g.* "the best and the brightest"), or mention the issue you are working on (e.g. "those spirits that are clear of any aspects of this specific problem"), etc.

5. **The *Invocation* connects all to the Divine Plan.**

   By harmonizing with the Divine Plan, you receive answers that are not only "for your highest and best good" (which the High Self/Soul Committee provides), but also weaves your answers with what is best for you in the overall scale of existence.

Using the Worksheet to Check for Preparedness

Before going further with a session, it is recommended to use the **LifeWeaving** worksheet and make sure that reciting the *Invocation* cleared what was needed. Test for a 'yes' or 'no' on the first 11 steps of the *Preparedness Checklist* and do **LifeWeaving** clearing on any 'no' answers.

If you have questions about what to clear and the lines of questions to use, the individual steps that take place during the Invocation are presented in detail in my book *Advanced Dowsing with the LifeWeaving System*.

The **LifeWeaving** Worksheet is available for free download at www.AyniLifeWeaving.com.

CHAPTER 4

Power Chart Section A

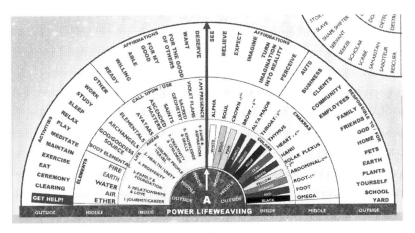

Figure 7 POWER CHART: *Section A*

Directional Ring

If dowsing the POWER *Chart Key* indicates *Section A*, to find your answer first move to the Directional Ring to test which row of information is needed: the inner (*Life Areas and Colors*), the middle (*Elements, Call Upon/Use* and *Chakras*) or outside (*Activities, Affirmations*, and *Responsible To/For*).

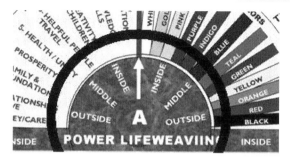

Figure 8 POWER *Section A*: Directional Ring

Life Areas

The various *Life Area* categories are borrowed from *Feng Shui,* the ancient Chinese practice focusing on the circulation and flow of energy to create balance and harmony in all areas of life.

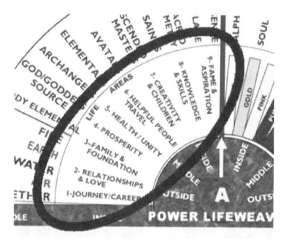

Figure 9 POWER CHART, *Section A: Life Areas*

The nine *Life Areas* are as follows:

1. **Journey/Career** - includes job satisfaction, your spiritual path, the way you approach things generally, and new beginnings and opportunities.

2. **Relationships/Love** - includes relationships with family, friends, business associates, and children. It includes the amount of commitment, attraction factors, and whether you feel depleted or not.

4 Southeast **Prosperity**	9 South **Fame,** **Aspirations**	2 Southwest **Relationships** **Love**
3 East **Family,** **Foundation**	5 **Health,** **Unity,** **Balance**	7 West **Creativity/** **Children**
8 Northeast **Knowledge/** **Skills**	1 North **Journey/** **Career**	6 Northwest **Helpful People,** **Travel**

Figure 10 *Feng Shui* Life Areas

3. **Family/Foundation** - includes long-term prosperity, your heritage, ancestors, parents, superiors, and other influences from the past. This is the foundation from which you operate, either consciously or subconsciously.

4. **Prosperity** - the flow of universal abundance in any form such as good health, material possessions, money, blessings, etc.

5. **Health/Unity** - the center section of the diagram, connects to our happiness and enjoyment of life as well as health and vitality. This area relies upon having all the other eight life areas balanced and in harmony.

6. **Helpful People/Travel** - indicates help from family, friends, colleagues, officials, strangers, or even opening a book and finding an answer to a question; it also refers to how you are helping others. Additionally this area can relate to travel.

7. **Creativity/Children** - relates to what you create or give birth to, including children, job or work creations, hobbies or opportunities in general.

8. **Knowledge/Skills** - includes all skills and inner knowledge. It is your educational level, studies, introspection, meditation, spiritual focus and guidance from your Soul Committee (High Self).

9. **Fame/Aspirations** - relates to the expression of your individuality, what lights you up in your life, and what you are known for. This area is also your spiritual enlightenment and self-realization. It includes things like charisma, life clarity, gossip, courage, and fears.

Colors

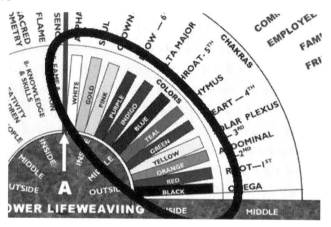

Figure 11 POWER CHART *Section A: Colors*

Sometimes either during or after a clearing, it is helpful to apply specific color frequencies to the chakras or body. If a color or colors are indicated during **LifeWeaving** clearing, add them to the 'basket' with the other words that are dowsed and clear as usual.

Color correction can also be accomplished by eating the right colored foods, wearing colored clothes, surrounding yourself with decorations or using crystals of a needed color, etc.

After a session or to help balance energy or emotions, the following therapeutic exercise for applying colors can be used with great success.

Therapeutic Color Exercise

a) Begin on the neutral line of the POWER LIFEWEAVING CHART *Section A: Colors*, letting the pendulum swing (spirit chooses) from one color to another as you think or say *"I surround myself in a bubble of ____ light and send that color around and through my body, through every organ and system, nerve, muscle, bone, even down to the cells and DNA."*

b) Throughout the exercise, as soon as the pendulum moves to a new color, mentally change the color of the bubble to the newly-indicated one and flood it through you, then to the next color and the next one, etc., until the pendulum stops at one color and remains steady or returns to the neutral line.

Note that if the pendulum lingers over one color longer than others, you should stay with that particular color until the pendulum moves to a new one. At other times the pendulum may only spend a second or two before switching. This entire color clearing process usually takes less than a minute.

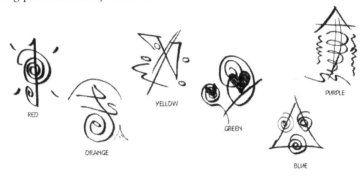

Figure 12 Energy Pictures Depicting Color Frequencies

The Elements

The *Elements* are the basic primary substances that, when mixed, give rise to various forms. Thus all objects of this world are related through the four elements and to the planets and stars. The continual changing relationship between these elements creates constant change in the human body as well.

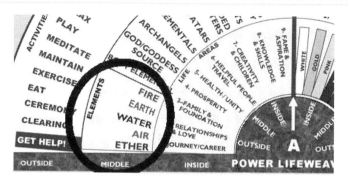

Figure 13 POWER CHART *Section A: The Elements*

1. **Ether** - the "*fifth element*" (the *quintessence*), was defined by Aristotle as having no qualities (neither hot, cold, wet, nor dry), was incapable of change (with the exception of change of place), and, by its nature, moved in circles. Think of ether as star energy. If you need more ether for balance, go out at night and absorb the energy from the starry heavens.

2. **Air** (thought) - an element of energy, breath, soul-minds, and liberation from the earth. The temperament of air is hot and moist, and its purpose in nature is to make things more delicate (finer and lighter) and thus more able to ascend into higher spheres. Air is also the agent by which breath moves in and out of the body and causes involuntary movements of the body.

3. **Water** (emotions) - this basic element is the most primary form in which liquid can exist; life-giving because liquids flow and move about. The addition of water allows the other elements to be shaped, molded, spread out and/or dispersed. The nature of water includes the focused energy of the will directed at the achievement of goals, the major developmental changes of life, as well as the limitations set by fear, inner strength and faith in self. Water needs to be contained or it will run unchecked and waste emotions. The water element is associated with both communication and emotions.

4. **Earth** (stability) - an element usually situated at the center of our existence. Earth's nature is at rest, and because of its inherent weight, all other elements gravitate toward it. Earth is typically

cold and dry in nature, as long as it is not changed by any other elements. The outward form of the body is fixed and held in place due to the earth element. An earth personality is rational, balanced, reliable, stable, practical, caring and concerned for others.

5. **Fire** (desire) - hot and dry in temperament, with the role in nature of rarefying, refining, and intermingling things. Fire has the power to penetrate and can ride through the element of air. It has the capacity to overcome the coldness of the two cold elements, earth and water, and so creates and maintains harmony among the elements. The nature of fire includes the spirit, consciousness, experience of unity in all life, love, affection and joy; communication and expression of ideas and feelings; spontaneous, lively and social.

Call Upon/Use

The *Call Upon/Use* section indicates where to turn to for help. When a Call Upon/Use answer is processed through the *Clearing Macro*, that specific energy (*e.g.,* Archangel, Elemental, Violet Flame, etc.) is applied to what is being cleared.

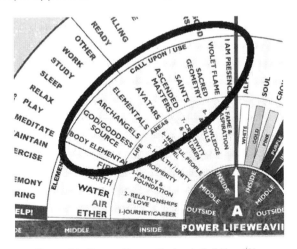

Figure 14 POWER CHART *Section A: Call Upon/Use*

1. **Body Elemental** - a special spirit in charge of maintaining a person's physical form throughout all lifetimes.

2. **God/Goddess/Source** - Totality.

3. **Archangels** - etheric world intelligences of a very high order who have always existed.

4. **Elementals** - life forms ranging from very low to very high forms of intelligences made of etheric world elemental essence; nature spirits.

5. **Avatars** - human beings who have perfected and purified their soul-minds through thousands of earthly incarnations to an exalted order in the angelic kingdom; they function to help the evolution of civilization.

6. **Ascended Masters** - human beings who have earned the rank of *Master*; abide on the fifth plane in the etheric world but choose to reincarnate into a physical body as a great leader to promote spiritual understanding and growth for civilization (*e.g.,* Buddha, Jesus, Krishna, Mohammed).

7. **Saint** - a person of great holiness considered to have earned an exalted place in the etheric world through the quality of his or her earthly lives, heroism, and ability to perform paranormal feats while living on Earth.

8. **Violet Flame** - the *Violet Flame* or *Violet Fire* transmutes unwanted conditions and balances all by the Light (associated with St. Germaine).

9. **Sacred Geometry** - is the symbolic and sacred meanings ascribed to certain geometric shapes and certain geometric proportions, used in the planning and construction of religious structures (churches, temples, altars and mosques, etc.), of sacred spaces (sacred groves, village greens and holy wells), and of the creation of religious art.

10. *I AM* **presence** - your own divine self.

Chakras

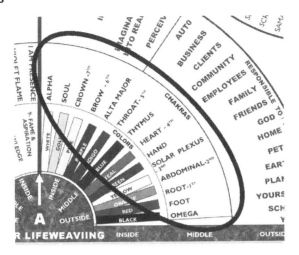

Figure 15 Power Chart Section A - Chakras

The *Chakras* comprise an invisible, inter-dimensional energy transducing system running up and down the spine, ultimately connecting our endocrine system with the energy fields surrounding us and converting that energy into usable body fuel. Each chakra resembles a swirling cone of energy, open in the front and back but very narrow in the center of the body. If you need more information to clarify an issue, the chakras are well-documented in Chapter 21 as to location, function, organs affected, association with physical and emotional problems, color, element, and corresponding points in Chinese medicine.

- Alpha Chakra
- Soul Chakra
- Crown Chakra (7th; Third Ear)
- Brow Chakra (6th; Third Eye; Pineal)
- Alta Major Chakra (Chandra; Mouth of the Goddess)
- Throat Chakra (5th)
- Thymus Chakra (Etheric Heart or High Heart)
- Heart Chakra (4th)
- Hand Chakras
- Solar Plexus Chakra (3rd; Power)
- Abdominal Chakra (2nd; Sexual; Spleen)

- Root Chakra (1st)
- Foot Chakras
- Omega Chakra

Activities

The *Activities* section shows what you should be doing to help a situation or where your energy should be directed at in a particular time.

- **Get help!** - stop working on yourself and ask for help from someone else (another dowser, a medical doctor, etc.). Consider this a spiritual 9-1-1 call to seek outside assistance.
- **Clearing** - indicates that you, your pendulum, and/or your environment are not clear enough to work and get reliable answers, or that the client or his or her environment needs cleared. Methods for clearing include smudging, prayer, a shower or bath, pendulum clearing, etc.

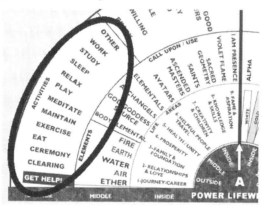

Figure 16 POWER CHART *Section A: Activities*

- **Ceremony** - time out for ceremony of some sort to quiet yourself or set the stage for your work. Ceremony can include *Feng Shui* cures, prayer, lighting candles or incense, etc.
- **Eat** - time to feed your body.
- **Exercise** - get moving through stretching, toning, an aerobic workout, walking, yard work, running, using special equipment, etc.

- **Maintain** - represents basic, routine activities that keep our lives functioning. Maintain can include cleaning, dusting, vacuuming, doing dishes, laundry, balancing the checkbook, shopping for groceries, walking the dog, etc.
- **Play** - what is "play" to you? What is enjoyable and fun? Examples might be to shop, socialize, create something, work on your car, play computer games, etc.
- **Relax** - how do you wind down from daily stress? What do you like to do to let go of tension? Examples might be reading, doing artwork, doing puzzles, watching TV/DVD, going to the theatre, taking a bath, getting a massage, etc.
- **Sleep** - get more sleep!
- **Study** - seek more knowledge.
- **Work** - if you run a business, your choices might include calling clients, working on finances, working on your website, ordering supplies, organizing, etc.
- **Other** - something not included on this chart.

Affirmations

Affirmations are declarations, "words of truth," traditionally aimed at the subconscious, that when recited often, can transform us from within and create desired outward manifestations.

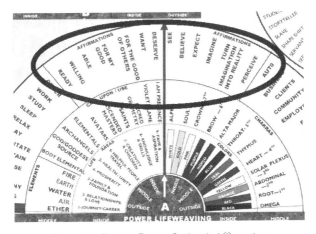

Figure 17 POWER CHART *Section A: Affirmations*

Affirmations Protocol

The affirmations can be used to test that you are totally clear of an issue or identify where a blockage pops up:

(1) Place your pendulum into a neutral swing over the POWER CHART *Section A* neutral line.

(2) Mentally add what you wish to test (*e.g.*, "exercise more").

(3) Add in each affirmation one at a time, and check for neutrality/no programs (the pendulum remains on neutral). For example, *"I am ready to exercise more; I am willing to exercise more; it is for my good and the good of others that I exercise more; etc."*

(4) If an affirmation is blocked (the pendulum moves off the neutral line), use intention and place the affirmation statement with the issue and the client on the *Chart Key* neutral line and do the *Basic LifeWeaving Protocol* to clear the block to neutrality.

(5) Repeat the affirmation and issue once more to confirm that it has cleared.

The affirmations are:

> *"I am ready to..."*
> *"I am willing to..."*
> *"I am able to..."*
> *"It is for my good..."*
> *"And for the good of others..."*
> *"I want to..."*
> *"I deserve to..."*
> *"I commit to..."*
> *"I see..."*
> *"I believe..."*
> *"I expect..."*
> *"I imagine..."*
> *"I turn imagination into the reality of..."*
> *"I perceive..."*

Responsible To/For

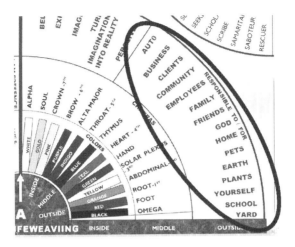

Figure 18 POWER CHART *Section A: Responsible To/For*

The *Responsible To/For* chart section alerts a person to whom or what they should be responsible to or for at any moment - something that many people have difficulty with. When POWER LIFEWEAVING, this section can be used independently for a quick reality check or coupled with the activity section. In the following list, each activity includes some suggestions - but feel free to add your own:

1. **Auto** - maintenance needed? washing? cleaning? gas? air for the tires?

2. **Business** - bookkeeping? advertising? cleaning? calls? scheduling for the future?

3. **Clients** - thank you notes? follow-up report? interviews? appointment confirmation?

4. **Community** - volunteering? clean-up? projects?

5. **Employees** - tardiness? harmony? reliability?

6. **Family** - needs? play? vacation? clothes? shopping?

7. **Friends** - calls? play? in need of help?

8. **God/Source** - meditation? clearing? honoring? belief?

9. **Home** - pick up? deep cleaning? rearrange? dusting?

10. **Pets** - health? feed? groom? playtime?

11. **Earth** - healing? being more green? smaller footprint?

12. **Plants** - feed? water? trim? repot?

13. **Yourself** - more rest? better food? more exercise? more private time? more socializing?

14. **School** - homework? paying attention in class? being on time? honoring teachers?

15. **Yard** - mowing? trimming? weeding?

CHAPTER 5

Power Chart Section B

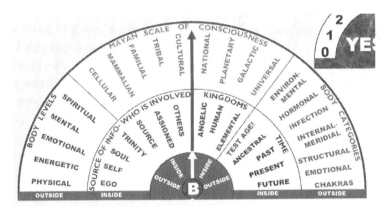

Figure 19 POWER CHART *Section B*

Directional Ring

By testing this section of the chart first, the dowser is directed to read either the inside row of information (*Source of Information, Kingdoms,* or *Time*) or the outer row (*Body Levels, Mayan Scale of Consciousness,* or *Body Categories*).

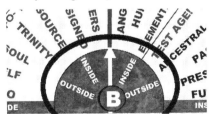

Figure 20 POWER CHART *Section B: Directional Ring*

Source of Information/Who is Involved

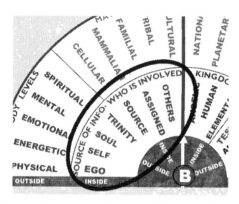

Figure 21 POWER CHART *Section B: Source of Information/Who is Involved*

Dowsing the *Source of Information-Who is Involved* section can show what part of the *Personal Trinity,* guides and/or guardian angels are involved in a program, as well as where answers are coming from. Checking for the source of answers is the most critical step to ensure accurate dowsing.

1. **Ego** - represents a combination of the conscious and subconscious mind. The Ego is established from all of one's past and present life experiences, as well as one's attitude toward those experiences. As a result, the Ego is very much interested in self-survival.

2. **Self** - is a fragment of the entire entity functioning to develop as a human being. It is who you are, what you think and what you feel, especially the conscious feeling of separation and being different from other people. When clearing physical issues, the Self often needs to be addressed separately after clearing the *Personal Trinity.*

3. **Soul (High Self)** - is the invisible life force of existence found in every living thing. The High Self can be thought of as a small group of higher-level beings, all actually part of the soul, looking out for a spirit's highest and best good, much like a nanny cares for her charges.

4. ***Personal Trinity*** - is the term used to indicate the harmonized Self, Soul and Ego.

5. **Source** - is all the power, all the love, and all the wisdom in the universe - an infinite soul and infinite spirit which is behind all things.

6. **Assigned Souls** - are God-sanctioned guardian angels and guides working with a person.

7. **Others** - can either be incarnated (a spouse, a doubting associate or a friend) or a spirit (good, bad or indifferent).

Three Kingdoms

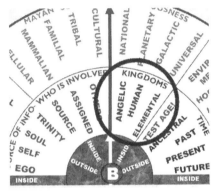

Figure 22 POWER CHART *Section B: Kingdoms*

Our world is comprised of three kingdoms - the human, elemental and angelic. These kingdoms should all be working in synchronicity. For the most part, however, they are not due to the human kingdom's use of free will and the universal law. The universal law states that *"beings in one dimension cannot assist beings on another dimension unless the request or invitation comes from the dimension wishing to receive assistance."* In order to take advantage of the resources offered by Three Kingdoms, we humans must learn to communicate and work in harmony with the other two.

1. **Human Kingdom** - Humans work with thoughts and feelings, taking and energizing ideas from the higher planes. Humans are generalists and emphasize free will.

2. **Elemental Kingdom** - Elementals work primarily on the mental

plane and are known as "builders of form." They translate thought forms into the physical. As specialists, the elementals represent the inner spiritual forces of the four elements.

Each elemental kingdom is under the direction of an elemental king, who serves one of the four great archangels. Elementals can evolve into devas (in charge of larger landscapes of the nature kingdom) and finally into gods (highly evolved elementals).

The elementals on this planet are sworn to materialize humanity's thoughts and feelings. Thus, disasters such as earthquakes, tornados, or factors such as pollution are at least partially due to human thought patterns.

Every human being also gets a personal body elemental who has volunteered to support his or her physical form each lifetime. It helps to send your personal body elemental gratitude, love and appreciation for centuries of dedicated service!

The elementals are:

- Earth Elementals - gnomes, elves, memehune
- Air Elementals - sylphs and fairies
- Fire Elementals - salamanders (not related to what we call lizards)
- Water Elementals - undines or mermaids

3. Angelic Kingdom - Angels administer to the spiritual and emotional needs of the Human and Elemental Kingdoms by primarily working on the emotional plane. Humans also have personal angels known as guardians.

Each Archangel is a specialist radiating one particular quality or virtue that has its own color, sound, fragrance and flame. For example,

- Archangel Michael's quality is faith and protection,
- Archangel Uriel's quality is the light and knowledge,
- Archangel Chamuel's quality is divine love and the adoration flame, and
- Archangel Raphael's quality is healing and consecration.

Angels create multi-angel force fields using sacred geometry and symmetrical patterns, which function as carriers of energies up and down between dimensions.

Time

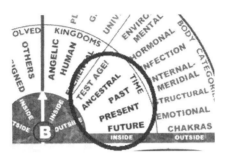

Figure 23 POWER CHART *Section B: Time*

The *Time* category on the POWER LIFEWEAVING CHART includes the following classifications:

- **Test Age!** - If this answer is dowsed, use any number chart to test for an age when a program originated. Once you know the age, if desired, you can also check the RESEARCH CHART to find the particular energy involved and any pertinent relationships connected to the initiation of that program. Place the age, relationships, energies and client's memories on the neutral line of the *Chart Key* and clear using the *Basic LifeWeaving Protocol.*

- **Ancestral** - the time of past generations, whose programs are carried forward in our DNA. To clear the DNA, apply the **LifeWeaving** findings to seven generations on both the mother's and father's sides. Clearing these programs also clears the entire line of descendants and siblings.

- **Past** - any past lifetime.

- **Present** - during the current lifetime.

- **Future** - time where programs are "yet to happen."

Body Levels

The vibrational bodies are important to clear since they often hold *engrams,* which are blocking memories of past traumatic events

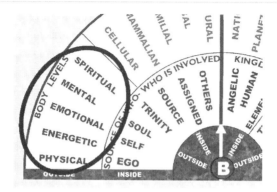

Figure 24 POWER CHART *Section B: Body Levels*

that will affect lifetime after lifetime until the lessons are learned and the blockages are cleared. The POWER LIFEWEAVING CHART uses one of the oldest and simplest explanations of the theory of these vibrational body levels.

1. **Physical** including its **Etheric** counterpart (an exact replica of the *physical* body) - the *physical* body is comprised of chemicals assimilated in a living field that gives it shape. At this body level, health problems materialize in the form of symptoms or discomfort significant enough to get our attention. The *etheric* body (considered the seat of all memory) serves as a pattern for future emotions and character traits. It also acts as a battery for the body's health and vitality by absorbing the life force given off by the universe through the chakra system. The physical body level is associated with the earth element and the etheric body is associated with the air element.

2. **Energetic** (or **Astral***)* - the astral body level, able to separate from the physical at will, acts as a link between the etheric and mental levels by receiving and transmitting energy vibrations. The astral body holds the emotions of the physical in memory form only and has no conscious mind, yet it is still subject to the Earth's desires and habits. This body is associated with the air element.

3. **Emotional** (includes the **Lower Mental-Causal, Buddhic** and **Atman** levels) - this body is directly linked to our emotions. The lower mental-causal body is where our intuitive feelings form,

acting as a storehouse for the essence of all experience gained through previous incarnations. The Buddhic level works with our Soul/High Self through intuition and inspirational thoughts. The Atman level acts as a strainer separating the waste of unnecessary reactions from karma now overcome. The emotional body levels are associated with the water element.

4. **Mental (Thought Body or Monad)** - the mental or monad body is considered to be the indestructible unit of our existence - a minute, ethereal, concentrated mass of energy and intelligence containing a complete replica of when it was in its original perfect state. The mental body is associated with the fire element.

5. **Spiritual** - the spiritual body represents layers of entities beyond an individual person, including the soul twin (the other half of the original soul after the first split into duality), soul and flame families (like-minded groups of spirits working together on various issues), and Source.

Mayan Consciousness Scale

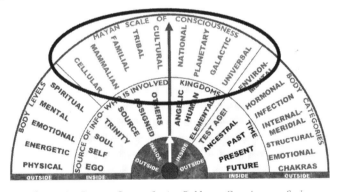

Figure 25 POWER CHART *Section B: Mayan Consciousness Scale*

The Mayan pyramids were monuments to creation as it unfolded and to both the Divine and humankind's place in time. These pyramids were referenced in the Mayan calendar as "step pyramids" because each step represented the ascension of human-kind. Each step shows a level of consciousness, from the beginning of existence to the now and even to the end of time. The Mayan levels of consciousness offer a unique way to research deeply ingrained energetic blocks.

The nine levels of the *Mayan Scale of Consciousness* are as follows:

1. **Cellular** - the first level of consciousness which started with the "Big Bang" over 16 million years ago.

2. **Mammalian** - second step of the pyramid starting 820 million years ago.

3. **Familial** - third level of consciousness of the rise of families and individuals that began 41 million years ago.

4. **Tribal** - the fourth step indicating the creation of tribal culture, two million years ago.

5. **Cultural** - the fifth level starting 102,000 years ago that was the beginning of the creation of human cultures on the Earth.

6. **National** - the sixth level when nation states were created (3115 B.C.), when writing began, and when agriculture began to flourish.

7. **Planetary** - the seventh level of consciousness when science and the industrial revolution began in 1775. This is the consciousness of the planet and all that live on, within, or over it.

8. **Galactic** - the eighth level of galactic consciousness level that began on January 5, 1999.

9. **Universal**—this final level of consciousness began on February 10, 2011 and ended on October 28, 2011.

Figure 26 Mayan Step Pyramid

Body Categories

The *Body Categories*, used to test the major systems of the body, are identical to the main categories found on the PRSM DIAGNOSTIC CHART. A physical complaint will often respond to a general clearing of the involved system without the need to research further.

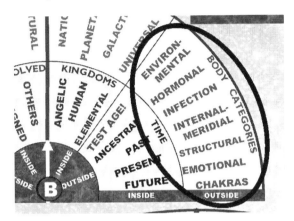

Figure 27 POWER CHART *Section B: Body Categories*

The main categories and subcategories of each body system are listed below:

1. **Environmental** - includes the subcategories of stress, allergies, electrical and/or magnetic, chemical, iatrogenic (being caused by the physician), nutritional, radiation, ley lines or toxic streams, and other.

2. **Hormonal** - includes gonads (sex organs), adrenals, liver, thymus, parathyroid, thyroid, hypothalamus, pituitary and other.

3. **Infection** - includes toxins, parasites, virus, bacteria, yeast or fungus, stones or sludge, AIDS or ARC (AIDS-Related Complex), cancer and other.

4. **Internal-Meridial** - includes all the internal organs - brain, EENT (ears, eyes, nose and throat)/sinus/teeth, heart, small intestine, lungs or bronchi, large intestine and appendix, spleen, stomach and pancreas, liver, gallbladder, kidney, urinary bladder, and endocrine. This list also correlates to the paired acupuncture meridians.

5. **Structural** - includes bones, muscles, skin/cells, lymph, nerves, diaphragms, and blood vessels.

6. **Emotional** - includes scars and blocks, chemical imbalance, and psychic attack.

7. **Chakra** - includes all the chakras including hands and feet. In depth descriptions are available in Chapter 21.

If further research is necessary to clear a problem, use the PRSM CHART.

CHAPTER 6

Power Chart Section C: Archetypes

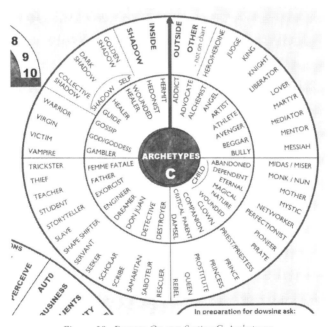

Figure 28   POWER CHART *Section C: Archetypes*

Introduction to Archetypes

The word archetype comes from the Greek *arche* meaning "basic," and *typos* meaning "type of form." Archetypes act as a universal memory bank, built by the mental activity of mankind since Earth began, and which man responds to unknowingly. This memory bank holds all the ideas, thoughts, images, patterns, community forms, etc. that are now an inheritance in everyone's subconscious mind. By tapping into this bank, mankind can react in a human manner. For example, everyone knows that a 'mother' should instinctually act as life-giver, nurturer, and a source of unconditional love, patience and caring. This is the framework for every mother's behavior although each individual fills in the actual details of the experience.

Plato defined archetype as a basic form or pattern, like a prototype, on which all objects of a certain category are built.

Carl Jung used the word archetype more to represent the collective unconscious. He said *"There are as many archetypes as there are typical situations in life. Endless repetition has engraved these experiences into our psychic constitution, not in the forms of images filled with content, but at first only as forms without content, representing merely the possibility of a certain type of perception and action."*

In her book, *Sacred Contracts*, Carolyn Myss refers to archetypes as "energy companions" and encourages everyone to recognize and integrate these archetypal patterns into their awareness. This can help a person understand sources of fears, reactions, behaviors and perceptions.

Joseph Campbell pointed out that we should see the archetypes as blueprints for handling specific situations that we will encounter during our lifetime.

Shadow Aspects of the Archetypes

In a world of polarity, we would say that archetypes have both light and dark aspects. The shadow aspects, which are mostly rooted in fear, appear to represent that part of ourselves that we are least familiar with. Shadows come from both emotional and psychological patterns of repressed feelings that we do not want to deal with.

Jung calls the *Shadow Self* "that which we think we are not." It is considered to be the "threshold between the ego and subconscious mind," holding the parts of us that we reject and want to keep hidden. This *Shadow Self* grows from negative thoughts and feelings, and becomes an entity comprised of everything the ego finds unacceptable. We are born with it and we will die with it.

The *Shadow Self* can fit into one of three categories:

- **Dark Shadow** - all the negatives we want to hide. *Dark Shadow* traits can include archetypes like *pirate, saboteur, critical parent, slave, victim, clown*, etc.
- **Golden Shadow** - positive traits such as accepting power or being a great leader that we love and admire but cannot ever imagine that it can be a part of us. The *Golden Shadow* might include such archetypes as *hero, mentor, warrior, scholar* or *angel.*
- **Collective Shadow** - these aspects are universal. For example, a religion may carry the *Collective Shadow victim* archetype as part of its identity, or doctors might carry the *god* archetype.

If we take on a shadow archetypal role, we usually do not make the best decisions or have the best motivation and often use it to sabotage ourselves. As a result, we need to learn to get along with a shadow aspect - much like we have learned to get along with our ego - by giving it attention, giving in, resisting, and talking to it. The *Shadow Self* can be a tremendous teacher if we allow it to be more a part of our conscious mind and take responsibility for it. However, realize that no fear is stronger than our own *Shadow Self*, and the defenses we adopt to avoid confrontation are huge.

The following suggestions can help you gain control of and heal your *Shadow Self*:

- Have the courage to look at your *Shadow Self* while maintaining a strong ego and self-esteem. Be aware of the shadow and its affect on your life.
- Be humble.
- Name the shadow and maintain a humorous attitude about it.
- Own your shadow and look at it without rejection. You created your own life, including the shadows. Take the knowledge of any undeveloped resources that it offers you.

- Have the patience to rebuild who you are and respect any previous defenses you put up. Shadows are not evil!
- Do not try to fix other people's shadow!

The Role of Archetypes in Dis-ease and LifeWeaving Clearing

Archetypal patterns are important to address in healing work because they govern both the conscious and subconscious minds and, in turn, the body and emotions.

By dowsing for the specific archetype a person is using in any given situation, one can better understand where a person is both consciously and subconsciously coming from. For example, in a strained relationship between a married couple, the husband might see his wife as the *perfectionist* or *critical parent* archetypes, while the wife might see her husband as a *dreamer*. These descriptive labels can be a key to understanding the real trouble in that marriage and offer clues as to how to best address the problem.

In another example, someone dealing with an illness may be running the *damsel* archetype waiting for a *knight* (*healer*) to save him or her rather than engaging in self-healing activities.

Archetypes can also become a problem if the "tape" gets stuck in the subconscious and locks a person into a particular way of acting or reacting that does not allow for any flexibility. For example, if a little girl's father acts like a *critical parent*, that child might start using the *femme fatale* archetype to deal with him, using her "feminine wiles" to wrap him around her finger and distract his critical approach. Later in life, this grown woman may automatically go into the same archetypal response each time she encounters a man or anyone being critical.

During a LifeWeaving session, I often find that even after all programs between two people seem to be cleared, one (or both) may still be holding onto either a conscious or subconscious archetypal pattern of the other. If these are also not addressed, a blockage will simmer between those involved - not the neutrality that we desire - and issues will start to rebuild.

LifeWeaving clearing can bring a person into neutrality with no preconceived archetypal pattern in mind. From this point of neutrality, he or she can choose, as needed, any particular archetypal pattern that would most effectively deal with a particular situation.

After clearing karmic issues or programs between people, it is good to test for any conscious or subconscious archetypal patterns that might still be lurking between them. This can prevent programs from rebuilding.

Protocol for Testing that Archetypes have been cleared

1. After completing clearing work between people, place one of them on the POWER CHART *Archetypes Section* neutral line. This will test his or her point of view.
2. Ask, "*How does this person consciously see the other?*"
3. If the pendulum remains in a neutral swing, the clearing is done. If an archetype does indicate archetype(s), take the results to the POWER *Chart Key* and do **LifeWeaving** clearing until neutrality is reached.
4. Next ask, "*How does this person subconsciously perceive the other?*"
5. If "neutral," the clearing is done. If an archetype comes up, take it to the POWER *Chart Key* and do **LifeWeaving** clearing until neutrality is reached.
6. Repeat steps 2 - 5 for the other person involved until neutrality is reached for both.

Using the Archetypes Chart Section

The Archetypes section includes two alphabetically-arranged circles of commonly encountered archetypes. All of these are described in detail later in this chapter.

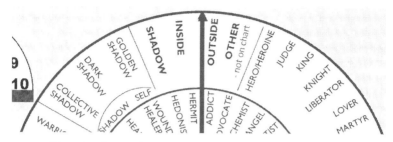

Figure 29 POWER CHART *Section C*: Top of the Archetypes Chart

The inside and outside categories at the top of the *Archetypes* section help the dowser decide whether to use the inside or outside circle of answers.

If *Shadow* tests (at the top left of the section), it acts as an adjective to the archetype that tests next. For example, shadow + lover = *shadow lover*.

After identifying an archetype, if you wish you can move to the RESEARCH CHART *Section A Keyword Petals* for specific *Keywords* identified with that archetype. That information is usually not necessary to clear the archetype yet can be helpful when an archetype has many variations. For example, a *queen* might be bad (the Ice Queen in The *Chronicles of Narnia*, the evil queen in *Sleeping Beauty*) or good (Arwen in *Lord of the Rings*, Elsa the snow queen from *Frozen).*

Archetype Definitions and Energy Pictures

The following pages include the definitions, examples and energy pictures of all archetypes shown on the chart.

ADDICT
(WORKAHOLIC, GLUTTON, GAMBLER)

The *Addict* archetype is extremely devoted to him or herself or to the habitual self-application of something. The addiction can be to anything. The *Addict* shows that an outside force is stronger acting than inner spirit. It is willpower vs. self-control.

Examples: Kurt Cobain; Kenny Rogers in *The Gambler*.

ADVOCATE
(ATTORNEY, DEFENDER, LEGISLATOR, LOBBYIST, ENVIRONMENTALIST)

This archetype is an intercessor, defender or counselor; its work involves public expression and social change. The *Shadow Advocate* works on causes for personal gain or negative issues.

Examples: Timothy Leary; Al Gore; Kevin Trudeau; Jimmy Carter.

Shadow Examples: Keanu Reeves and Al Pacino in *The Devil's Advocate.*

ALCHEMIST (WIZARD, MAGICIAN, SCIENTIST, INVENTOR)

The **Alchemist** archetype transmutes substances. The **Shadow Alchemist** tends to misuse its power and knowledge.

Examples: Juliette Binoche as Vianne from *Chocolat;* Professor Dumbledore in the *Harry Potter* movies; Johnny Depp in *Edward Scissorshands*.

Shadow Example: Willy Wonka.

ANGEL (FAIRY GOD-MOTHER/ GODFATHER)

An **Angel** archetype is a guardian spirit or attendant. The **Shadow Angel** misuses its power to control or mislead others.

Examples: Oskar Schindler; Roma Downey in *Touched by an Angel*; Nicholas Cage as Seth in *City of Angels*; John Travolta in *Michael*; the Fairy Godmother in *Cinderella*.

Shadow Example: Silas in *The Da Vinci Code*.

ARTIST
(MUSICIAN, AUTHOR, ACTOR, CRAFTSPERSON, POET, SCULPTOR, WEAVER)

An *Artist* archetype is creatively skilled at doing something well.

The *Shadow Artist* is overly eccentric and egotistical.

Examples: Andy Warhol; Paul McCartney; Georgia O'Keefe; Tom Hulce in *Amadeus*.

Shadow Example: Van Gogh; Picasso.

ATHLETE

The *Athlete* archetype demonstrates physical strength and agility as expressions of the strength of the human spirit.

The *Shadow Athlete* misuses its power or has a false sense of invulnerability.

Examples: Hercules; Daniel Day-Lewis in *My Left Foot*; Geena Davis, Madonna and Rosie O'Donnell in *A League of Their Own*.

Shadow Examples: Tanya Harding; Mohammed Ali; Tom Selleck in *Mr. Baseball.*

AVENGER
(AVENGING ANGEL, SAVIOR)

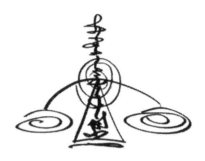

The **Avenger** is one who needs to balance the scales of justice.

The **Shadow Avenger** resorts to violence.

Examples: Perry Mason; David Carradine in *Kung Fu*; Emma Peel and John Steed characters from *The Avengers.*

BEGGAR
(HOMELESS PERSON)

The **Beggar** is an impoverished pauper, depending on others for its needs. **Beggar** is a test of self-empowerment starting at the level of physical survival.

Examples: *Oliver Twist* by Charles Dickens; Patrick Swayze in *City of Hope*; many televangelists.

BULLY
(COWARD)

A person who is quarrelsome, swaggering and cowardly, the **Bully** shows up as an archetype if someone is always facing experiences that are more powerful than him or herself.

Examples: Josef Stalin; J. Jonah Jameson from *Spider Man*; Jack Nicholson in *As Good as It Gets*; Bert Lahr in *The Wizard of Oz*.

CHILD

In general, the **Child** archetype is young and immature, having major issues about life, safety, nurturing, loyalty, and family.

The **Shadow Child** is concerned with only its own well-being.

Note that there are many more archetypes describing the **Child** that are not listed below but the following listed below are the most common.

CHILD, ABANDONED / ORPHANED

The *Abandoned Child* is not part of a family psyche or tribal spirit so he or she survives by developing personal judgment and experience.

The *Shadow Orphan* reveals abandonment and rejection and seeks out surrogate families such as therapeutic groups.

Examples: Bambi; Hayley Mills in *Pollyanna*; Macaulay Culkin in the early *Home Alone* movies.

Shadow Examples: Harry Potter; Little Orphan Annie.

CHILD, DEPENDENT

The *Dependant Child* relies heavily upon others for guidance and support.

Example: Matthew McConaughey in *Failure to Launch.*

CHILD, ETERNAL

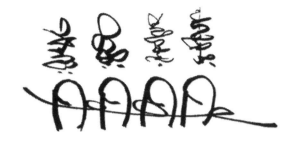

The *Eternal Child* always strives to be eternally young and enjoy life.

The *Shadow* refuses to grow up and be responsible or becomes dependent on someone who will care for its physical needs.

Examples: Robin Williams in many of his roles; Tom Hanks in *Big*.

Shadow Example: Peter Pan; Steve Martin as Navin R. Johnson in *The Jerk*.

CHILD, MAGICAL
Innocent Child

The *Magical Child* shows the enchanted and enchanting parts of a child, and holds a belief that anything is possible.

The **Shadow** of this archetype is a lack of belief that miracles can happen, often times bringing out depression and pessimism or retreating into fantasy.

Examples: Anne Frank; Tiny Tim in *A Christmas Carol*; Drew Barrymore in *E.T.*

Shadow Example: Charlie Brown.

CHILD, NATURE

The **Nature Child** has a deep bonding with nature and animals.

The **Shadow Nature Child** may be abusive to animals, people and the environment.

Examples: Tarzan; Timmy in *Lassie*; Elizabeth Taylor in *National Velvet*; Maya Dolittle in *Dr. Dolittle 3*.

CHILD, WOUNDED

The **Wounded Child** has had abusive childhood experiences, placing blame for current problems on those abuses. This archetype has a strong desire to help others with their wounds and to walk a path of forgiveness.

The **Shadow** can fall into self-pity.

Examples: Natalie Wood in *Miracle on 34th Street*; Linda Blair in *The Exorcist*; *Oliver Twist* by Dickens.

CLOWN

The *Clown* archetype is zany—a jester who makes people laugh or cry, and always wears a mask. The *Clown* uses humor to work with power.

The *Shadow Clown* is cruel and often betrays those who have trusted him.

Examples: Ellen DeGeneres; Charlie Chaplin; Buster Keaton; Jim Carrey; Jackie Chan; Robin Williams; Tom Hanks in *Forrest Gump*.

Shadow Example: The Joker in *Batman*.

COMPANION

Companion archetype is the comrade, associate or mate, who offers emotional support, loyalty, tenacity and unselfishness.

The **Shadow** side often shows betrayal.

Examples: Robin from *Batman*; Tinkerbell; Dr. Watson with Sherlock Holmes; Tonto in *The Lone Ranger*.

Shadow Example: Gollum in *Return of the King*.

CRITICAL PARENT

This archetype shows severe judgment and fault finding.

Example: Johnny Cash's father from *Walk the Line*.

DAMSEL (PRINCESS)

The *Damsel* is usually a beautiful and vulnerable young maiden in need of rescue. After rescue by her knight, she is cared for lavishly.

The *Shadow Damsel* encourages patriarchal dominance over the weak and helpless female.

Examples: Elizabeth Taylor; Robin Wright in *The Princess Bride*; Princess Leia from *Star Wars*; Kate Winslet from *Titanic*.

Shadow Example: Katharine Hepburn in *African Queen*.

DESTROYER
(MAD SCIENTIST,
SERIAL KILLER,
SPOILER)

A person running the archetype of **Destroyer** ruins, dissolves and ends things in order to rebuild.

The **Shadow** obsesses with and becomes addicted to its own destructive power.

Examples: Fred McMurray in *Son of Flubber*; Sylvester Stallone in *Rambo;* Walter Pidgeon as Morbius in *Forbidden Planet*.

Shadow Examples: Stalin; Mao; Anthony Hopkins in *Silence of the Lambs*.

DETECTIVE
(SPY,
PROFILER)

The **Detective** is the investigator archetype, having great powers of observation.

The **Shadow Detective** can become a voyeur, falsify information or sell out to the highest bidder.

Examples: James Bond; Sam Spade from *The Maltese Falcon*; Peter Falk in *Columbo*; Inspector Clouseau from *The Pink Panther*.

Shadow Example: Mata Hari.

DON JUAN
(GIGOLO, SEDUCER, SEX ADDICT)

Like **Femme Fatale**, the **Don Juan** is the male archetype and uses sexual energy for power, preying on women for the sake of conquest only. Within the **Don Juan** there does exist an underlying vulnerability with the power to open a heart.

Examples: Johnny Depp from *Don Juan de Marco*; Richard Gere in *American Gigolo*.

DREAMER
(VISIONARY)

The **Dreamer** is a dreamy and impractical archetype; it sees possibilities beyond the scope of individual life, benefiting all.

The **Shadow Visionary** may alter the vision to make it more acceptable to others or to sell out to the highest bidder.

Examples: Muhammad; Howard Hughes; Matthew Broderick in *Ferris Bueller's Day Off*.

Shadow Example: Jim Jones.

ENGINEER
(ARCHITECT, SCHEMER, MANAGER, DESIGNER, PLOTTER, BUILDER)

The *Engineer* archetype demonstrates a practical hands-on approach, devoted to making things work.

The *Shadow Engineer* can become a master manipulator for its own needs.

Examples: Frank Lloyd Wright; Howard Hughes; Jeff Bridges in *Tucker*.

Shadow Example: Alec Guinness in *Bridge on the River Kwai*.

EXORCIST
(SHAMAN)

The *Shaman* conjures or summons an evil spirit and releases it.

The *Shadow Shaman*, however, never has courage to face its own demons.

Examples: Van Helsing from *Dracula*; Bruce Willis in *The Sixth Sense*; Ghostbusters.

Shadow Examples: Hyde in *Dr. Jeckel and Mr. Hyde*; Richard Chamberlain in *The Thorn Birds*.

FATHER
(PATRIARCH, PARENT)

The *Father/Paternal* archetype has the ability to oversee others, offering courage and protection.

The **Shadow Father** becomes dictatorial and abusive.

Examples: Andy Griffith; Captain von Trapp in *The Sound of Music*; Homer Simpson; Ben Cartwright in *Bonanza*.

Shadow Example: Darth Vader in *Star Wars.*

FEMME FATALE
(BLACK WIDOW, FLIRT, SIREN, SEDUCTRESS)

Femme Fatale uses her feminine wiles to dominate, but also has a tendency to kill the object of her affection. This archetype does open the heart.

Examples: Lauren Bacall; Sharon Stone; Marilyn Monroe; Elizabeth Taylor in *Cleopatra*; Kathleen Turner in *Body Heat.*

GAMBLER

Gambler is a compulsive risk taker trying to outrun the odds as well as following its own hunches.

Examples: Paul Newman in *The Hustler*; Steve McQueen in *The Cincinnati Kid*; Wesley Snipes in *White Men Can't Jump*; Kenny Rogers as *The Gambler*.

GOD/GODDESS

This is the archetype of the exalted being; the ultimate in dominance; possessing a lifelong sense of power.

The *Shadow God/Goddess* can be a dictator, exploiting that power.

Examples: George Washington; Zeus; Aphrodite.

Shadow Examples: Cleopatra; Marlon Brando in *The Godfather*.

GOSSIP

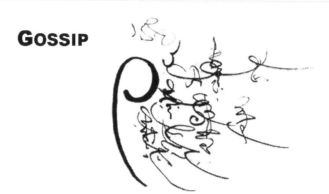

Gossips thrive on idle chatter, passing rumors and secrets. The *Gossip* is backbiting and often exaggerates information, using it to disempower others. Integrity, honor and trust are the lessons of the *Gossip* archetype.

Examples: Joan Rivers; Jerry Springer; John Malkovich and Glenn Close in *Dangerous Liaisons.*

GUIDE (GURU, SAGE, WISE WOMAN, PREACHER, SPIRITUAL MASTER)

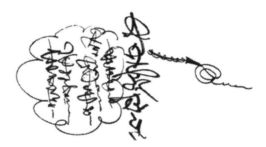

A *Guide* archetype shows the way, directs or leads to a spiritual level.

The *Shadow Guide* wants to control its followers and create financial gain.

Examples: Master Po in *Kung Fu;* Pocahontas.

Shadow Example: Gollum in *Lord of the Rings,* Jim Jones.

HEALER (NURSE, CAREGIVER, THERAPIST, COUNSELOR)

The *Healer* archetype offers cures, remedies or repairs for health issues.

Examples: ET; nurse Colleen McMurphy in *China Beach*; counselor Deanna Troi in *Star Trek: The Next Generation*.

HEALER, WOUNDED

The *Wounded Healer* archetype becomes a healer by way of its own personal hardship, healing only through self work.

Like the *Shadow Healer*, the *Shadow Wounded Healer* tends to take advantage of those they are working with.

Examples: Chiron; Hawkeye in *MASH.*

Shadow Example: Kathy Bates in *Misery*.

HEDONIST (GOURMET, CHEF)

A *Hedonist* archetype has gross self-interest, exaggerating and overindulging in pleasures without regard for its health or for the good health of others.

Examples: Dean Martin; Jabba the Hut in *Star Wars*.

HERMIT

The **Hermit** archetype is one who abandons society and chooses to live alone.

Examples: J. D. Salinger; Howard Hughes; Obi-Wan Kenobi in *Star Wars*.

HERO/HEROINE

A *Hero* or *Heroine* archetype displays valor, fortitude, and courage.

The **Shadow** version empowers itself at the cost of others.

Examples: Superman; Peter Parker in *Spider Man*; Wonder Woman; Sigourney Weaver in *Alien*; Kirk Douglas in *Spartacus*.

Shadow Example: General George Custer.

JUDGE (CRITIC, MEDIATOR, ARBITRATOR)

The *Judge* archetype is invested with the authority to decide the merits of things. The **Shadow** shows consistent criticism and lacks compassion.

Examples: Judge Judy and Judge Wapner from TV; Spencer Tracy in *Judgment at Nuremberg*.

Shadow Example: Judge Roy Bean.

KING
(EMPEROR, RULER)

The *King* archetype, a male sovereign ruler of a kingdom, displays the height of male power and authority.

The *Shadow King* resists criticism and believes fully in entitlement.

Examples: King Arthur; Yul Brenner in *The King and I*.

Shadow Examples: Colonel Kurtz from *Apocalypse Now;* Marlon Brando in *The Godfather*.

KNIGHT
(WARRIOR, RESCUER)

The *Knight* archetype is loyal and honorable, reminiscent of a self-sacrificing gentleman bred to the profession of arms.

The *Shadow Knight* may lack honor and loyalty, and may save others without paying attention to his own needs.

Examples: James Bond; Bruce Wayne/Batman; Shrek; Harrison Ford as *Indiana Jones*; Antonio Banderas in *The 13th Warrior*.

Shadow Examples: Kamikaze pilots; the Crusaders.

LIBERATOR

The *Liberator* archetype is the one who sets others free or releases them from bondage and injustices.

The *Shadow Liberator* sets others free but then imposes its own tyranny.

Examples: Gandhi; Abraham Lincoln; Robin Hood.

Shadow Examples: Simon Bolivar; Nikita Khrushchev; Anthony Quinn in *Zorba the Greek*.

LOVER

Lover archetype is a warm admirer; a passionate and devoted friend; one who loves. This archetype is connected to self-esteem and appearance.

The *Shadow Lover* has an exaggerated, obsessive passion that becomes destructive.

Examples: Pepe le Pew; Woody Allen; Ingrid Bergman and Humphrey Bogart in *Casablanca*; *Beauty and the Beast*.

Shadow Example: Jessica Walter in *Play Misty for Me*.

MARTYR

The **Martyr** archetype gives service and dies or suffers for its principles.

The **Shadow Martyr** uses it as a means to manipulate and control its environment.

Examples: Meryl Streep in *Silkwood*; Ben Kingsley in *Gandhi*.

Shadow Example: General George Custer.

MEDIATOR (AMBASSADOR, DIPLOMAT)

The **Mediator** archetype reconciles differences between warring factions.

The **Shadow Mediator** has a hidden agenda, looking for personal gain out of the resolution.

Examples: Franklin Delano Roosevelt; Shirley Temple; Jimmy Carter.

Shadow Example: Thomas Cardinal Wolsey; Cardinal Richelieu from *The Three Musketeers*.

MENTOR
(MASTER, COUNSELOR, TUTOR)

A **Mentor** archetype is an implicitly trusted teacher, guide or friend.

The **Shadow Mentor** imposes more control than wisdom.

Examples: Socrates; Alec Guinness to Mark Hamill in *Star Wars*; Paul Newman to Tom Cruise in *The Color of Money*; Sidney Poitier to his students in *To Sir with Love*.

Shadow Example: The Emperor to Darth Vader in *Stars War*.

MESSIAH
(REDEEMER, SAVIOR)

The **Messiah** archetype is the anointed one; a looked-for divine liberator of a people.

The **Shadow Messiah** shows extreme obsession to the point of being dangerous to others.

Example: Jesus; Mohammad.

Shadow Example: Robert De Niro in *The Mission*.

MIDAS/MISER

The *Midas* archetype turns things into gold, having extreme creative ability as well as the need to control all forces around itself for fear of losing wealth.

The *Shadow Midas* falls into greed and begins to hoard, thus becoming a *Miser* - one who saves or greedily hoards.

Examples: Michael Douglas in *Wall Street*; James Dean in *Giant*.

Shadow Example: Scrooge in *A Christmas Carol.*

MONK/NUN (CELEBATE)

The *Monk* or *Nun* archetype is devoted to a life that is spiritually intensive, dedicated and persistent.

The *Shadow Monk* or *Nun* removes itself from the real world, and feels privileged to not worry about that world.

Examples: Audrey Hepburn in *The Nun's Story*; Deborah Kerr in *Heaven Knows, Mr. Allison*; Friar Tuck in *Robin Hood.*

Shadow Example: Cloistered monks and nuns.

MOTHER/ MATERNAL (MATRIARCH, MOTHER NATURE)

A *Mother* archetype is the female parent; the life-giver; the source of nurturing and caring; the keeper and protector of life. The *Mother* archetype includes several categories including *Perfect, Devouring, Abusive, Abandoning*, and *Working Mother*.

Examples: Myrna Loy in *Cheaper by the Dozen*; Anne Bancroft in *The Pumpkin Eater*; Mother Mary; Mother Goose; Irene Dunn in *I Remember Mama.*

MYSTIC

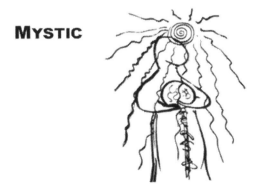

The *Mystic* archetype professes knowledge of spiritual truth or a feeling of union with the divine; it often pays the price of physical suffering and hard work to achieve this status.

The *Shadow Mystic* becomes very self-centered and self-important, and may take advantage of admirers.

Examples: St. Germaine; Joan of Arc; Merlin; Richard Dreyfuss in *Close Encounters of the Third Kind*

Shadow Example: Jim and Tammy Faye Bakker.

NETWORKER (MESSENGER, HERALD, JOURNALIST)

A *Networker* archetype forges alliances and connections with many different groups, thus enhancing social flexibility and empathy.

The *Shadow Networker* uses others for personal gain.

Examples: Oprah Winfrey; Jimmy Carter.

Shadow Example: Peter Finch in *Network.*

OTHER

Indicates some archetype not on this list. If you want a ballpark idea, ask to see what the closest archetypal option on the chart would be.

PERFECTIONIST

The *Perfectionist* archetype demands a high level of excellence in performance and behavior of all around him.

Examples: Tony Shalhoub as Adrian Monk in *Monk*; Charlton Heston as Michelangelo in *The Agony and the Ecstasy*.

PIONEER
(EXPLORER,
SETTLER,
ENTREPRENEUR,
PILGRIM)

Pioneer is an innovative archetype, discovering new things or places.

The ***Shadow Pioneer*** compulsively abandons the past and moves on.

Examples: Orson Welles; Valentina Tereshkova (first woman in space); Jody Foster in *Contact*; *Little House on the Prairie*; *Wagon Train*; *Bonanza*; *Star Trek*.

Shadow Example: Leonardo de Caprio in *Catch Me if You Can.*

PIRATE

The ***Pirate*** archetype is the thief of the open seas, usually robbing from the rich, then burying his or her treasure. To the poor, the pirate symbolizes freedom and an ability to strike back at the rich. Stolen treasure can either be money or the intellectual property of another.

Examples: Errol Flynn in *Captain Blood*; Johnny Depp in *Pirates of the Caribbean*; Stewart Granger in *Scaramouche.*

PRIEST/PRIESTESS (MINISTER, RABBI, SHAMAN)

The *Priest* or *Priestess* archetype is one who is especially consecrated to the service of a divinity, and serving as a mediator between the divinity and its worshipers.

The *Shadow Priest* cannot live by the rules that they set for others.

Examples: The Dalai Lama; Karl Malden in *On the Waterfront*.

Shadow Example: Richard Burton in *Beckett.*

PRINCE

A *Prince* archetype is the non-reigning member of a royal family, and is in training to be of service to those he will rule.

The *Shadow Prince* seeks power for himself without regard to the needs of others.

Examples: *The Prince and The Pauper*; Robert Redford in *The Way We Were*.

Shadow Example: Paul Newman in *Cat on a Hot Tin Roof.*

PRINCESS

The **Princess** archetype is the damsel in the castle, surrounded by comfort, awaiting rescue from the **Knight**. She looks out for her own comfort but also the welfare of others.

The **Shadow Princess** expects others to do what she should be doing for herself.

Examples: Princess Leia in *Star Wars*; *Sleeping Beauty, Cinderella.*

Shadow Example: Kate Capshaw in *Indiana Jones and the Temple of Doom*.

PROSTITUTE

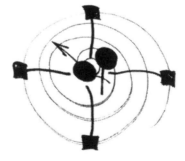

The **Prostitute** *is an* archetype using seduction and control as a means of survival. By selling itself out, it loses self-esteem and self-respect.

Examples: Marlon Brando in *On the Waterfront*; Jack Lemmon in *Save the Tiger*; Shirley MacLaine in *Irma la Duce*.

QUEEN

The *Queen* archetype is the female sovereign or monarch; she represents power and authority.

The *Shadow Queen* shows aggression and destructive patterns of behavior, especially if she feels she is being challenged. The *Shadow Queen* archetype includes *Ice Queen, Queen Bee,* and *The Dark* or *Evil Queen.*

Examples: Mary (Queen of Heaven); Judi Dench in *Shakespeare in Love*; Cleopatra; Evita Perone; Queen Elizabeth.

Shadow Example: The Ice Queen in the *Chronicles of Narnia*; the queen in *Sleeping Beauty*.

**REBEL
(REVOLUTIONARY,
NONCONFORMIST,
PROTESTER)**

The *Rebel* archetype resists authority and helps others break out of tribal patterns.

The *Shadow Rebel* may reject legitimate authority out of personal dislike.

Examples: The Founding Fathers; Kirk Douglas in *Spartacus;* Meryl Streep in *Silkwood;* Sally Field in *Norma Rae.*

Shadow Examples: James Dean in *Rebel Without a Cause*; Peter Fonda (Wyatt) and Dennis Hopper (Billy) in *Easy Rider; Thelma and Louise.*

RESCUER

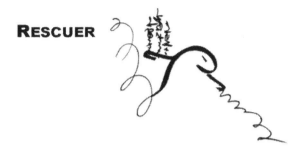

The **Rescuer** archetype saves, supports or frees another, and then withdraws.

The **Shadow Rescuer** - usually feminine - engages in emotional support with the hidden agenda to get love in return.

Examples: *The Lone Ranger*; Alan Ladd as *Shane*; Tom Hanks in *Saving Private Ryan*.

Shadow Example: Queen Elizabeth I.

SABOTEUR

The **Saboteur** archetype is one who creates mischievous damage, suffering from fear and low self-esteem, blocking its own empowerment and success.

The **Shadow Saboteur** uses self-destructive behavior or tries to undermine others.

Examples: *Amadeus* as presented by author Peter Shaffer; Max Smart in *Get Smart*.

Shadow Example: Angela Lansbury in *The Manchurian Candidate.*

SAMARITAN

The *Samaritan* archetype displays humanity and compassion to someone it is least inclined to serve.

The *Shadow Samaritan* helps someone to the detriment of itself.

Examples: Paul Newman; Liam Neeson in *Schindler's List*; Richard Dreyfuss in *Down and Out in Beverly Hills*.

Shadow Example: Tom Hanks in *Saving Private Ryan.*

SCHOLAR

Scholar archetype displays an enthusiasm for learning.

The *Shadow Scholar* is an eternal student—one who cannot transfer its acquired knowledge into living in the real world.

Example: Noah Wylie as *The Librarian* (after landing his job).

Shadow Example: Noah Wylie as *The Librarian* (before landing that job).

SCRIBE
(SECRETARY, ACCOUNTANT)

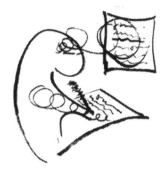

The **Scribe** archetype writes or copies rather than creating new documents or ideas.

The **Shadow Scribe** alters facts, plagiarizes, or sells information that belongs to others.

Examples: Bob Cratchit from *A Christmas Carol*; Dustin Hoffman and Robert Redford in *All the President's Men*.

Shadow Example: Nicole Kidman in *To Die For.*

SEEKER
(WANDERER, NOMAD)

The **Seeker** archetype searches or questions out of curiosity. At its core, the **Seeker** is searching for God anywhere wisdom may be found.

The **Shadow Seeker** becomes aimless, ungrounded, and disconnected from any goal and others.

Examples: Harrison Ford as *Indiana Jones*; Michael Palin; Brad Pitt in *Seven Years in Tibet*; *Siddhartha* by Herman Hesse.

Shadow Example: A religious recluse.

SERVANT

The *Servant* archetype works for or assists another.

The *Shadow Servant* forgets to be of service to itself at the same time.

Examples: Cinderella; Morgan Freeman in *Driving Miss Daisy*.

Shadow Example: Igor from *Frankenstein*.

SHAPESHIFTER

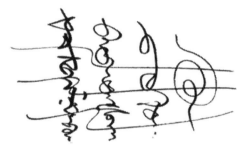

The *Shapeshifter* archetype changes appearances readily and navigates through different layers of consciousness.

The *Shadow Shapeshifter* may be unstable, fickle, and have a lack of conviction.

Examples: Benjamin Franklin; Madonna; Howl in *Howl's Moving Castle*; Tony Randall in *The Seven Faces of Dr. Lao*; Chuck Norris in *Forest Warrior*.

Shadow Example: Peter Sellers in *Dr. Strangelove*; Tom Ripley from *The Talented Mr. Ripley*; Woody Allen in *Zelig*.

SLAVE
(PUPPET)

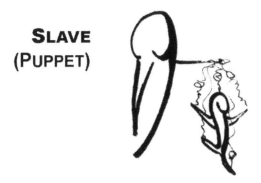

A *Slave* archetype portrays one's will or person being held by another and has no power of choice or self-authority.

Examples: Russell Crow in *The Gladiator*; Victor Mature in *The Robe*; LeVar Burton in *Roots*; Ossie Davis in *Slaves*.

STORYTELLER
(MINSTREL,
NARRATOR)

The *Storyteller* archetype relates stories, which include a metaphoric learning or experience.

The *Shadow Storyteller* can exaggerate or lie to gain an advantage for itself.

Examples: Joseph Campbell; Peter Falk in *The Princess Bride*; *Lord Jim* by Joseph Conrad.

Shadow Example: Scheherazade in *The Arabian Nights*.

STUDENT
(DISCIPLE, FOLLOWER, APPRENTICE)

The *Student* archetype is engaged in a course of study.

The *Shadow Student* falls into misusing the information it is learning, or never puts its learning to use.

Example: Luke Skywalker in *Star Wars*.

Shadow Example: Mickey Mouse as *The Sorcerer's Apprentice* from *Fantasia.*

TEACHER
(MASTER, PROFESSOR)

The *Teacher* archetype gives lessons to others.

The *Shadow Teacher* intentionally holds back information as a means of controlling others, for self-controlling interests, and/or for being needed.

Examples: Yoda and Obi-Wan Kenobi from *Star Wars*; *Our Miss Brooks*.

Shadow Example: David Hasselhoff in *Click*.

THIEF (CON ARTIST, SWINDLER)

The *Thief* archetype takes something physical, emotional or intellectual from others (symbolically implying a need for self-respect).

Examples: *Robin Hood*; James Caan in *Thief*; Abu in *The Thief of Baghdad*; Steve Martin and Michael Caine in *Dirty Rotten Scoundrels.*

TRICKSTER

The *Trickster* archetype plays practical jokes and pranks. This archetype can offer alternatives to the straight and narrow path that life offers.

Examples: The Joker from *Batman*; Kokopelli.

VAMPIRE

A **Vampire** archetype preys upon others for nourishment, showing strong codependency.

Examples: Bela Lugosi in *Dracula*; *The Vampire Chronicles* by Anne Rice; Rasputin.

VICTIM

The **Victim** archetype sacrifices itself or is sacrificed, often through passivity, rash or inappropriate actions.

The **Shadow Victim** enjoys the role for the sympathy it receives from others.

Examples: Marilyn Monroe; John F. Kennedy; Hillary Swank in *Boys Don't Cry*.

Shadow Examples: Laura Palmer from *Twin Peaks*.

VIRGIN

The **Virgin** archetype symbolizes purity or the beginning of creation or of ideas.

The **Shadow Virgin** has prudish disgust with, or fear of, sensuality.

Examples: Mother Mary; Kenneth from *30 Rock*; the Vestal Virgins; Sean Connery in *The Medicine Man*.

Shadow Example: Elizabeth I.

WARRIOR (SOLDIER, MERCENARY, AMAZON)

A **Warrior** archetype engages in battle, and has the ability to protect, defend and fight for one's rights. This archetype is considered invincible and loyal.

The **Shadow Warrior** seeks victory at any cost.

Examples: Dan Millman in T*he Peaceful Warrior*; Mel Gibson in *The Road Warrior*; *Xena, Warrior Princess*; *Buffy the Vampire Slayer*; *Wonder Woman,* Tom Cruise in *Mission Impossible*.

Shadow Example: *The Terminator*; Ronon Dex from *Stargate Atlantis;* the Ice Queen in *Chronicles of Narnia.*

Figure 30   **LifeWeaving** the Archetypes

THE LIFEWEAVING

RESEARCH CHART

CHAPTER 7

LifeWeaving and the Research Chart

Introduction

The RESEARCH CHART works in conjunction with POWER LIFEWEAVING to find additional details about what is being cleared. Identification of the type or origin of a problem, who is involved, what questions to ask, as well as the specific energies affecting issues or conditions for people, pets, businesses or problems can be obtained from the RESEARCH CHART.

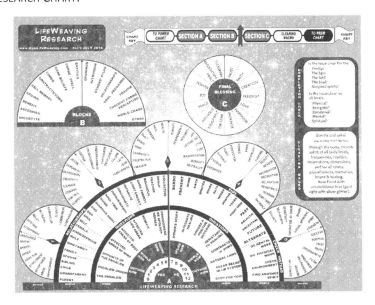

Figure 31 RESEARCH LIFEWEAVING CHART

As our frequencies have increased over the past few years, the research details for clearing have become less important. However, learning more about a problem can still help the client and/or practitioner in understanding what is going on as well as in finding related avenues that need to be cleared.

The RESEARCH CHART can be used to identify certain information such as blocks, to identify or clarify relationships, to find what questions to ask, or to find descriptive Keywords.

Another reason to use this chart is when dowsing during a **LifeWeaving** session, the *Chart Key* on one of the other charts (PRSM or POWER) indicates the dowser should go to the RESEARCH CHART.

RESEARCH CHART Protocol

1. Place the harmonized *Personal Trinity* of the person being tested plus their issue on the RESEARCH *Chart Key* neutral line and dowse for your next action.

2. Move to the neutral line of the indicated section and begin dowsing, allowing time for your pendulum to show as many answers as possible. Mentally or verbally add those *Keywords* to an imaginary "holding basket."

3. When your pendulum returns to and remains on the section neutral line, it indicates that the section is complete.

4. Return to the RESEARCH *Chart Key* neutral line and dowse for the next section needed (if any). Continue to follow steps 1 - 3 as *Keywords* come up until *Clearing Macro* is indicated and the contents of the holding basket are processed. Note that the *Clearing Macro* may come up on this chart or you may be directed to return to the POWER or PRSM CHARTS for additional items.

5. Do the *Completion Check* to be sure all parts of the *Personal Trinity* and that all body levels are clear.

6. Spiral unconditional love (gold light with glitter) through the body, mind and spirit to fill in where energy was removed.

7. You can now ask that the healing work just completed be moved through seven generations for both parents, siblings and descendants, then followed with unconditional love.

8. Take the original statement being cleared back to the POWER CHART and test for neutrality.

9. Finally make sure there is nothing else by asking *"Is there anything else contributing to the issue?"* or *"Is there anything else I should check instead?"* If the pendulum remains in neutral or indicates *"No,"* the session is done.

CHAPTER 8

Research Chart Section A

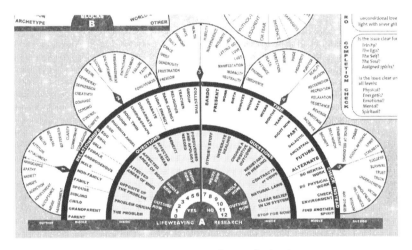

Figure 32 RESEARCH CHART: *Section A*

The **LifeWeaving** RESEARCH CHART can be used in conjunction with POWER LIFEWEAVING or independently to conduct pendulum research. The various elements of *Section A* are included below.

Yes and No

This section is used to establish basic *"yes"* and *"no"* answers. Note that your pendulum should follow the chart regardless of what a normal *"yes"* or *"no"* would be if you were dowsing without a chart.

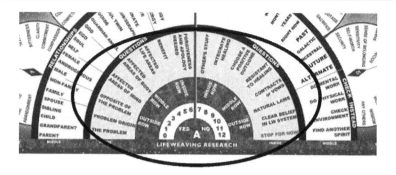

Figure 33 RESEARCH CHART: *Yes-No, Numbers, Directional Ring, Questions*

Numbers

The numbers can be used as 1 - 10, 1 - 100, 100 - 1000, etc.

Directional Ring

The dowser uses this section to test for which row: inside (*Questions*), middle (*Relationships, Time, Check Instead*), or outside (*Keyword Petals*) of information to read for the answer.

Dowsing Questions

Because knowing what to ask is one of the most difficult problems with dowsing, questions were added to the RESEARCH CHART to help spotlight the many potential aspects of a problem. The *Questions* portion of the chart will be indicated when working with the *Chart Key*. Also it can be used to see what to ask next or as a double check to make sure that you have addressed as many aspects of an issue as possible.

However, note that you can usually clear all these issues without further research. Simply add any questions that dowse positive to the "holding basket" with any other *Keywords* that come up, and spiral them through the body using the *Clearing Macro*. If a question still tests positive, test further. If you do go deeper, take any positives through the basic *Basic LifeWeaving Protocol*.

1. **The Problem** - Ask *"What is the problem?"* or *"What is going on?"*

2. **The Problem Origin** - Ask *"What is the origin of this problem?"* The origin (when the problem first cropped up) can be from a lifetime or experience that may seem to have nothing to do with what is currently happening. We go through many lifetimes working on variations of the same issue until we finally "figure it out" and get it cleared.

3. **The Opposite of the Problem** - Ask *"What is the opposite of this problem?"* When the opposite energy spirals through the body, it can help layer in a potential solution to the problem.

4. **Affected Areas of the Body or Mind** - Ask as a yes/no question *"Are any parts of the body or mind being affected by the problem?"* Follow up with the PRSM CHART and/or the basic **LifeWeaving** chart if the answer is *"yes."*

5. **Affected Areas of Life** - Use the POWER LIFEWEAVING CHART *Life Areas* on *Section A* and ask *"What areas of life are being affected by this problem?"* Clear any positives using the *Basic LifeWeaving Protocol.*

6. **Benefit** - Ask as a yes/no question *"Is there some benefit to having this problem?"* Follow up with **LifeWeaving** Clearing if *"yes."* A human being will often create, then encourage or hold onto a problem because of some perceived benefit to having it. The problem may create desired attention; keep you from doing something a part of you doesn't want to; alert you to some connected karma that still needs to be cleared, etc.

7. **Forgiveness or Apology Needed** -Ask as a yes/no question. *'Is there forgiveness or an apology needed?"* If *"yes,"* call for any souls that were or are involved to a neutral place (I use a "sandbox in the sky") and offer an apology and ask for forgiveness. We tend to hold on to the anger, resentment, entitlement issues, etc. since so many of our current issues resulted from violent past life confrontations with other souls. The important thing to remember is that it takes two to create conflict.

8. **Other's Stuff** -This indicates that the problem or statement you are clearing does not belong to the client. Go the *Relationships Section* of **LifeWeaving** RESEARCH CHART *Section A* and test *"Who does this problem belong to?"* and clear them and the problem. Also look for and clear any contracts, heart vows or hidden vows that the client might have that are attracting "others stuff."

9. **Integrate healing** - Ask as a yes/no question and look for energies that may be blocking integration. It also may take more time for integration of the clearing already done, or it may require taking time away from the clearing process to re-center and feel what is changing.

10. **Choose a Positive Outcome** - Ask *"Is there anything blocking a positive outcome from the clearing work?"* This is another way to ferret out a benefit program.

11. **Resistance to Healing** - Ask *"Is there resistance to healing the problem?"* You may feel at some level that you need to hold on to the problem - perhaps due to karma not yet cleared or obtaining a happy feeling with the attention the problem brings to you. If "yes," look for and clear *Keywords*.

12. **Contracts or Vows** - Ask as a yes/no question *"Are there contracts or vows involved in the issue?"* If *"yes"* destroy them and any backup copies in any way you desire. We often carry past life vows and contracts that no longer apply to our present life circumstances and they need to be removed. For example, in one lifetime as a monk you took a vow of poverty and that may still be affecting your current finances.

13. **Natural Laws** - Make allowances for natural physical laws (such as gravity) that affect our physical bodies. Believe in miracles but also allow for the natural laws that are part of the human experience on this planet.

14. **Belief in the LifeWeaving System** - Ask as a yes/no question (or you can test for the percentage of belief). If *"no,"* or less

than 100%, use *"This method infinitely helps"* as your statement to be cleared to 100% with **LifeWeaving**. If either you or the client doesn't believe that this method (or any other you are using) can help, it won't be nearly as effective.

15. **Stop for Now** - Ask *"Is it time to stop?"* If *"yes,"* take a break. If *"no,"* you may continue. Oftentimes when we learn a new method, we want to keep working until everything is cleared or completed. There is a time to stop and allow for releasing and integration.

Relationships

The *Relationships Section* includes many possible combinations found both in the physical as well as in the spiritual realm. Be aware that a person can test as having issues between his or her own Self, Ego or Soul as well as with another person or spirit.

Most relationship problems stem from past lifetime experiences and the cell memories that surface during a new lifetime. Clearing past karma between two people can have tremendous positive impact on present day interactions.

The following list includes relationship options found on the RESEARCH CHART. Note that some translation might be needed to understand; *e.g.,* a "parent male" can be a father, a policeman, or a male teacher.

1. Parent - person with some authority; mother or father.

2. Grandparent - person of stature and in authority.

3. Child - someone with little authority.

4. Sibling - brother or sister.

5. Spouse - marriage partner.

6. Family - group of related persons.

7. Non-family - group of non-related persons.

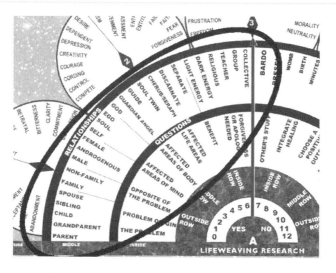

Figure 34 RESEARCH CHART *Section A: Relationships*

8. **Male** - male energy or sex.

9. **Androgenous** - balanced male-female energy.

10. **Female** - female energy or sex.

11. **Self** - human self portion of the *Personal Trinity*.

12. **Soul** - spiritual portion of the *Personal Trinity*.

13. **Ego** - child-like portion of the *Personal Trinity*, concerned with self-preservation and safety.

14. **God** - Source, the Divine, All That Is, Supreme Being of the Universe.

15. **Guardian Angel** - spirit assigned to offer protection.

16. **Guide** - spirits brought on to offer expert guidance.

17. **Soul Twin** - perfect match from the original soul split.

18. **Cherub/Seraph** - high ranking angels.

19. **Discarnate** - ghost.

20. **Separate** - vigilante-type ghost of higher vibration; has its own agenda and does not work through the *High Self/Soul Committee*.

21. **Light energy** - positive force portion of duality.

22. **Dark energy** - negative force portion of duality.

23. **Religious** - dealing with Source.

24. **Teacher** - instructing others.

25. **Group** - people connected in some way.

26. **Collective** - group consciousness. Check for and clear the reasons (especially contracts or vows) why the client is attracting these issues to themselves.

To Test: By dowsing you can identify a person's role in a past life or an individual's present life involvement. Let your pendulum select as many options as needed. For example:

> Parent + male + female = father and mother.
>
> Sibling + female = sister.
>
> Separate + dark energy = a dark energy entity.

Target Results: This section is used primarily to obtain more information. However, any programs between involved parties should be cleared.

Time

To Test: Place the harmonized *Personal Trinity*, the statement being cleared, and your pendulum on the neutral line of the RESEARCH CHART *Section A* and ask *"When did the program first originate?"* If it moves to Present Life, you can further research to identify specifically when it occurred during this lifetime.

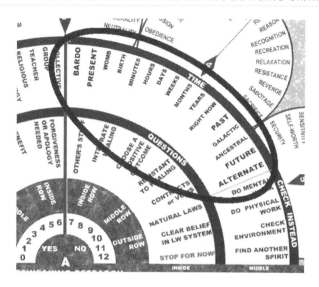

Figure 35 RESEARCH CHART *Section A: Time*

Target Result: No expectations.

To Clear: No clearing necessary—this section is used only to obtain more information—unless you are doing timeline clearing. Protocols for timeline clearing (entire lifetimes, specific ages, and past life time locks) can be found in my book, *Advanced Dowsing with the LifeWeaving System.*

Discussion: Times located on the right hand section of the RESEARCH CHART *Section A*, span from bardo to present life (womb to years to now) for researching when a life problem originated or reoccurred.

1. **Bardo** - time/place where our spirit exists between lifetimes.

2. **Present** - present lifetime issue. For further clarification, ask *"When was the program first established (womb to right now)?"* and *"At what specific age (how many minutes, days, months or years old was the person)?"* If the pendulum moves instead to an answer in the minutes to years categories, ask for *"How many?"* using the number section to obtain an answer for present life at a specific age, *e.g.* two months old.

3. **Womb** - period of gestation time in the mother.

4. **Birth** - time during the process of delivery.

5. **Minutes**

6. **Hours**

7. **Days**

8. **Weeks**

9. **Months**

10. **Year**

11. **Now** - current moment in time.

12. **Past** - any past lifetime other than 'galactic.'

13. **Galactic** - past life time at the very beginning when the star races began incarnating. Many of our karmic programs originated here.

14. **Ancestral** - the time of our ancestors, whose programs are carried forward in our DNA. Clearing this type of program extends healing to the entire line of ancestors and descendants.

15. **Alternate** - time in an alternate reality. Clear any alternate reality issues that are happening to the client, and ask spirit to *"Remove him or her from that existence if it is appropriate and bring the filtered energy back to the present life."* Also, send a team of angels to help complete the alternate life experience and work with those left behind. Note that some people are still working in two or, rarely, three concurrent lives.

16. **Future** - time in the future where programs are "yet to happen." Clear any future programs using *Basic LifeWeaving Protocol.*

Check Instead

If your pendulum indicates an item in the RESEARCH CHART *Section A, Check Instead*, that something is interfering with the clearing, and a different approach is needed to accomplish healing.

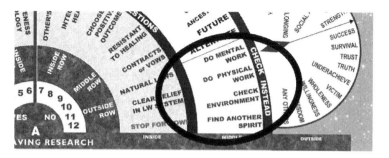

Figure 36 RESEARCH CHART *Section A: Check Instead*

1. **Do Mental Work** (such as counseling, hypnosis, etc.) - applicable if the client is having difficulty accepting this method of work, and might require a healing approach more in line with his or her own belief system. **LifeWeaving** results can be negated by a strong belief that it doesn't work. Also, results will not always hold without effort on the client's part to make personal life changes such as not using drugs or avoiding certain people or activities. The practitioner can also help to change the client's mental outlook through **LifeWeaving** clearing by using "*mental outlook*" as the issue to be cleared.

2. **Do Physical Work** - arises when direct attention to the physical body level is needed to ensure complete healing. **LifeWeaving** essentially works from the spiritual end of the healing spectrum and moves towards the physical, so a more physical approach can enhance the entire healing process. Modalities such as acupuncture, Reiki, massage and various energy work techniques can be extremely helpful. If a dis-ease is firmly manifesting on the physical level, alternative or Western medical intervention like surgery in addition to the energy clearing is often necessary.

3. **Check the Environment** - is basically the process of *Feng Shui,* where something in the environment is contributing to the problem. The major indication of an environmental problem is (1) the client gets better yet always seems to regress, (2) experiences improvement while on vacation away from home but gets worse upon returning, (3) if a person continually needs to be cleared of dark entities, there is a substantial possibility that the

home has openings (spirit gates) often due to clutter and dishar-mony. To effectively clear these spirit gates, three things need to happen: (1) the opening must be closed using intention, (2) the spirits that have traveled through the gate need to be cleared out (ask Archangel Michael's team to do this), and (3) the clutter needs to be removed. The *Life Areas* section in the POWER CHART *Section A* can be used to determine where a problem resides so the client can find and fix them.

4. **Find Another Spirit** - reveals the presence of another entity and/or group of entities that are either causing or adding to the problem. These entities can be incarnated, spirit, or both. Ask Archangel Michael's team to *"Find, clear and remove them."* Also test whether there are any reasons (such as *"curses, contracts, heart vows, hidden vows or soul programs')* attracting or holding entities to the client in the first place. Clear any positives with the *Basic LifeWeaving Protocol.* Note also *"Are any assigned spirit helpers involved?" 'How many?"* As needed do an *"Educate, elevate, remove or replace"* to clear and upgrade all spirit helpers.

The Keyword Petals

The *Keyword Petals* act as the heart of the RESEARCH CHART by helping to translate an issue, action, event, etc. into a matching word frequency or frequencies needed to clear or nullify a blocking energy, or to add in a necessary frequency that is missing.

The words found in the *Keyword Petals* help describe specific memories or actions that we hold in our bodies from the past, present and possibly the future. Sometimes the words seem completely relevant, while other times they do not make any sense at all. Simply trust that they need to be added in and do so.

The intent with LifeWeaving clearing is to nullify an issue by adding in the exact vibrational frequency of an emotional blockage in order to bring the client to a state of neutrality. For example, if a person is experiencing low back pain and your dowsing tests *Keywords* like *abuse, resistance, sacrifice and self-worth*, these frequencies indicate a "lack of support" emotional blockage that needs to be cleared, not just sore muscles. *Keywords* provide a different way to understand and address a presenting problem or symptom and represent lifetimes where experiences were either too pronounced or in excess, where there was an insufficiency or lack, or any level in between.

Another way the *Keywords* work is to add in an energy that is needed to help heal an issue. For example, in the low back pain case, the practitioner might also dowse the *Keywords* of *health, power, success, strength and clarity,* energies that will be retained during the spiraling action of the *Clearing Macro.*

Other times the dowsed *Keywords* include influences like the *Three Kingdoms, Saint* or *Avatars,* or various colors (found on the POWER CHART) that will also assist the healing process.

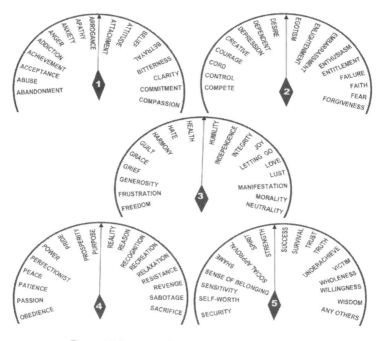

Figure 37 RESEARCH CHART *Section A: Keyword Petals*

CHAPTER 9

Research Chart Section B: Blocks

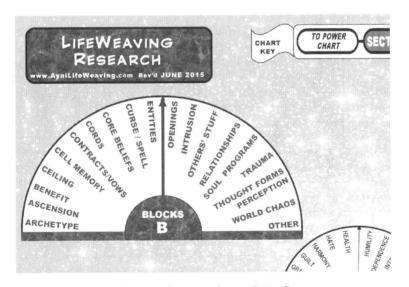

Figure 38 RESEARCH CHART: *Section B*

Introduction

The *Blocks Section* includes various ways that unwanted emotions lock into the body and mind, thus preventing optimum performance. These emotional energies usually start with a distasteful, painful or emotional incident from a past or current life that is unresolved. If not eventually addressed and cleared, the negative emotional stress resurfaces and a similar experience occurs—often in subsequent lifetimes. Eventually these negative emotions surface as unwanted behavioral patterns or muscle tension and pain resulting from blocked energy, blood or fluids in the physical, etheric, emotional, mental, or spiritual bodies. A person needs to become aware of that blockage and address and resolve it in some lifetime or the lesson will keep repeating.

Several types of blocks are listed below, including programs that a person might be running (*e.g., Soul Programs, Contracts/Vows, Benefit*) as well as outside influences that can block the smooth flow of life (*e.g., Cords, Curse/Spell, Entities/Openings, Intrusion, Trauma*, etc.). As you work, don't get caught up with the blocks as further research is not needed unless a block fails to clear. Just put them into the 'holding basket' for clearing. If a block does not clear easily, go to the POWER CHART, place the block and the client on the neutral line and proceed with the *Basic LifeWeaving Protocol*.

Types of Blockages

- **Archetype Blocks** - when a person locks into one particular way of thinking or acting, either towards him/herself or another person, ignoring all other possibilities. Think of archetypes as universal job descriptions that hold all the ideas, thoughts, images, patterns, community forms, etc. in everyone's subconscious mind. When we deal with people, we should start out in neutrality with them rather than being locked into a particular archetype.

- **Ascension Blocks** - currently being experienced by most of us since Earth is going through its seventh ascension attempt and all the previous attempts ended badly. Cellular memories of past ascension endings are beginning to trigger as we move through this current shift.

- **Benefit Blocks** - when a person creates, encourages, or holds onto a problem because of some perceived benefit to having it. The benefit block may create desired attention or may give an excuse not to do something.

- **Cell Memory Blocks** - due to a protoplasmic unit in each cell that compares to a human brain, and holds memories of every vibrational frequency a person has ever experienced. These units can die and be reborn from memory in subsequent lifetimes, and these memories can then lead to potential health issues and pain.

- **Contracts/Vows** (retract any vows and destroy all contracts using intention and **LifeWeaving Clearing**):

    o **Contract** - a past bargain or promise that is oftentimes made under duress, and is ultimately an unhealthy choice. Contracts should be rethought, reformulated or destroyed, and original contracts rescinded—especially those from past lives.

    o **Vow (Heart Vow or Hidden Vow)** - a serious promise, usually carried over from a previous lifetime, that is inappropriate in a person's current situation. For example, in one lifetime a soul acting as a priest takes a vow of poverty and then never seems to be able to make enough money in subsequent life experiences because that poverty vow is still in effect.

- **Cords** - energy conduits or lines sent by someone else (close by, distant, over the phone, or even from a past life) that attach to a person and severely drain his or her energy like a vampire sucking blood. The person doing the cording can either be very needy and may not be conscious of his or her act, or may be doing it on purpose. The person being corded will experience an intense, sudden drop in energy - feeling fine one minute and barely able to keep his or her eyes open the next.

When cords move through the *Clearing Macro*, the following occurs: a spiritual medical team removes the cords and heals the area; next the cord is ignited like a fuse with a flame of forgiveness and unconditional love, and then it burns back to the sender.

- **Core Beliefs** - develop throughout childhood due to life experiences. Core beliefs are the very essence of how we see ourselves, other people, the world, the future. They are strong and inflexible, and cause us to focus on only that which supports our beliefs.

- **Curse/Spell Blocks**:
  - **Curse** - the transfer of an evil psychic energy onto someone or something through the use of an elemental. A curse can either be sent by someone or may be boomeranging back to a person that cursed another in the past. This could have happened while being tortured or torturing someone else (which is why offering and asking for forgiveness as well as apology for ALL involved souls is so important). Using the POWER LIFEWEAVING *Clearing Macro* retracts the curse and applies forgiveness. Recorder Angels also re-write the scenario for the Akashic Records so all the involved souls can choose to accept clearing and break free of any effects of a curse.
  - **Spell** - a period of time during which a person or object is held captive by a psychic for the benefit of the psychic. The spell-bound person has limited freedom of mobility and thought.

- **Entities/Openings Blocks**:
  - **Entities** - the whole of something existing, animate or inanimate. As used here, an entity indicates an incarnated person, the collective, or a spirit. A *discarnate* entity is a ghost, usually trapped on this plane. A *separate* entity is a spirit that has crossed over but returns to this plane to complete its own agenda. Any of these beings can have either "light" or "dark" energy or hold a combination of both.
  - **Openings** - gates that allow spirits to easily enter our reality. Openings are often caused by chaos and clutter in the environment or by engaging in activities such as the use of recreational drugs. Send the entities and/or openings through the *Clearing Macro,* and ask Archangel Michael's team of

helpers to close and seal any openings, and to clear any spirit traffic that came through while a gate was open.

- **Intrusion** - active psychic weapon imbedded in a person's energy field. As the intrusion is sent through the *Clearing Macro*, a healing team of spirits is sent in to identify, clear and repair the area.
- **Others' Stuff** - what is coming up during testing is not really a problem for the person being tested but refers to the energy of the collective or some other soul. A person may have a contract or vow to run programs for others, or may just be extremely empathic. Sending *other's stuff* through the *Clearing Macro* should clear whatever is needed. Note to also check the client for any reason that he or she is running *other's stuff*. Rule out and clear as needed any *"curses, contracts, heart vows, hidden vows or soul programs."*
- **Relationship Blocks** - can be either family or non-family, from this life or other lifetimes in the past. The *Clearing Macro* addresses whatever is needed on a basic level to eliminate this type of block.
- **Soul Programs** - specific issues that a soul chooses to work on during a lifetime. This type of program often repeats in some form over several lifetimes until the person reaches a level of conscious-ness that opens knowledge of its existence, along with the desire and ability to address and finally clear the issue.
- **Trauma Blocks** - cellular imprints called engrams that form at the time of an accident or occurrence. These imprints can affect those involved for many years or over many lifetimes.
- **Thought Forms / Perception Blocks:**
  - o **Thought Forms** - intense thoughts or emotions expressed on a physical level that can linger in an area for years. According to Besant and Leadbeater in their book *Thought Forms*, this is "a living entity of intense activity animated by the one idea that generated it."
  - o **Perception** - the *Merriam-Webster Dictionary* defines percep-tion as "the way you think about or understand someone

or something; a mental image." For healing purposes, this energy layer is found very close to the physical level of a person but is not truly part of them, making perception more difficult to clear. This perception layer often needs to be addressed separately after clearing an issue on the other body levels.

- **World Chaos** - the craziness and disorder found on our planet at any given time. The presence of this block indicates that it is causing problems for the client, perhaps due to his or her increased sensitivity (empathy).

- **Other Blocks** - any other blocking issues not specifically listed on the chart.

CHAPTER 10

Research Chart Section C: The Blessing Seal

The Blessing Seal

The *Blessing Seal* statement was channeled by advanced lightworker John Allen. If we move beyond the limited model of 12 dimensions being used for LifeWeaving testing, this statement vibrates at a frequency of 17th dimension, 12th octave.

The statement is

Trust your Faith
in the Creation
of Freedom,
Love and Happiness.
Within Patience,
Without Fear in Judgment.
Sealed in Peace, Joy
and the Power within.
Flourish enlightenment.

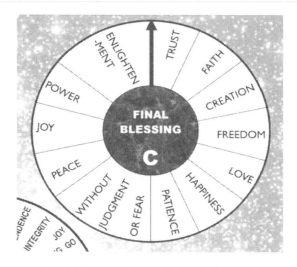

Figure 39 RESEARCH CHART *Section C: Blessing Seal*

Using the Blessing Seal

The *Blessing Seal* can be used in a variety of ways including:

1. You may be directed from the RESEARCH *Chart Key* to dowse the *Blessing Seal* in order to find pertinent *Keywords* that need to go into the "holding basket" as part of a clearing.

2. You can "*ask for a message from spirit*" and dowse the *Blessing Seal*. For example, a message of "*trust and patience*" might come up as a response indicating a need for both.

3. Simply apply the *Blessing Seal* at the end of each **LifeWeaving** session.

CHAPTER 11

Completion Check and Clearing Macro

The two elements used to complete a LifeWeaving clearing are the *Clearing Macro* and the *Completion Check*.

Bundle and spiral
(ALL WORDS THAT TESTED)
through the body, mind & spirit; at all body levels, frequencies, realities, incarnations, dimensions, and for all times; plus all blocks, memories, intent & healing. Now flood with unconditional love (gold light with silver glitter).

Figure 40 RESEARCH CHART: *Clearing Macro*

The *Clearing Macro*

A *macro* is defined as "large or long in size or duration." In computer work, a macro signifies "a single computer instruction that results in a series of instructions in machine language." In LifeWeaving the *Clearing Macro* contains a string of pre-set conditions that are invoked as the macro is recited.

The **LifeWeaving** *Clearing Macro* was developed as a means to quickly address exceptions that often showed up during a clearing, and to eliminate many of the double checks originally required.

Consider this the *"Michael Clearing Macro"* as a reminder that you are not the one doing the clearing. Instead, Archangel Michael and his team are actually interfacing with whatever needs to be cleared.

Each part of the *Clearing Macro* does a specific thing:

- **All Body Levels** - addresses any of the vibrational bodies, from the physical to the mental, or beyond to anything on the spiritual level (soul mates, flame family, etc.) that are being cleared.

- **All Frequencies** - makes sure that any blocking word vibrations are removed.

- **All Dimensions** - includes any situations from the lower 3rd through the 12th dimensions.

- **All Incarnations** - clears all times when a person existed in any physical form.

- **All Realities** - an "individual concept" of one's self and one's inhabitant, constructed by the mind of the individual. That which is real to the subconscious mind or psychic being regardless of actuality.

- **For All Times** - includes any past, present or future lifetimes.

- **All Blocks, Memories, Intent and Healing** - sending this phrase along with the bundle of dowsed *Keywords* catches anything extra.

- **And Infuse With Unconditional Love"** - replaces the energies that are removed with the superior energy of love.

Clearing Macro Protocols

During a **LifeWeaving** session, have the client imagine a "holding basket" to catch the identified *Keywords* as they are dowsed. Let the person know that spirit remembers what the words are, so he/she does not try to identify with them.

There are two ways to use the *Clearing Macro*:

1. Bundle all **LifeWeaving** findings together and simply say *'Apply the Clearing Macro.'*

2. Use intention or say out loud *"Bundle all the Keywords together and spiral them through the spirit, mind and body at all body levels, all frequencies, all dimensions, all incarnations, all realities, for all times. Then infuse with Unconditional Love* (gold light with glitter).

Completion Check

The *Completion Check* can be used each time you do the *Clearing Macro* but, better yet, wait until you feel an issue has been totally cleared. Then perform this check.

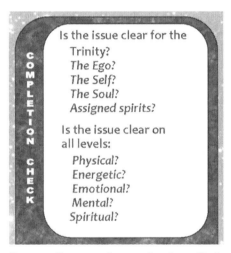

Figure 41 RESEARCH CHART: *Completion Check*

Therefore, to check for complete clearing:

1. Consider your first round of questioning to be for the client's *Personal Trinity* (the harmonized Ego, Self and Soul).

2. After an issue tests clear on the *Personal Trinity* level, place your pendulum into a neutral swing over a neutral line and ask *'Is the issue clear for the Ego?" "the Self?" "the Soul?"* If the pendulum moves off neutral for any of these questions (or you get a "*no*" answer),

the issue is not clear. Take that issue plus the level that tested as not clear, to the POWER CHART for the *Basic LifeWeaving Protocol.*

If necessary, clear any positives to neutrality by going back to either the POWER or RESEARCH CHARTS and using the issue (*e.g.,* back pain) + the level that is out of balance (*e.g.,* emotional). Clear to neutrality (*Personal Trinity* on all levels).

However, if testing the *Personal Trinity* shows there is still a problem on the Self level for example, take the issue + the Self to the POWER CHART and retest "*What is going on?*" and clear as needed.

3. After each part of the *Personal Trinity* and the assigned spirit helpers are cleared to neutrality, make sure the issue is also clear on the energetic, emotional, mental and spiritual levels in the same manner—use the neutral line and simply ask each to see if it is clear (pendulum remains in a neutral swing).

LifeWeaving
PRSM Chart

Disclaimer

LifeWeaving PRSM Diagnosis is not intended to replace standard medical care.

The accuracy as well as completeness of PRSM diagnostic research depends on the practitioner's dowsing skills and background knowledge.

Answers should always be taken in context with standard diagnostic methods as well as presenting symptoms, objective findings, the client's subjective feelings, along with a very large dose of common sense.

CHAPTER 12

Dis-ease, Energy and Medical Dowsing

The Theory of Dis-ease

Funk & Wagnalls Standard Dictionary defines disease as

- the disturbed or abnormal structure or physiological action in the living organism as a whole, or in any of its parts; a deviation from health, a state of balance and wholeness;
- a morbid condition resulting from such disturbance.

According to *The Donning International Psychic Dictionary*, disease is an energy field meant to bring

- pain, abnormal behavior or appearance, or incapacitation of normal functions, to remind one to change one's thinking (attitude), lifestyle, or both, to further soul-mind growth;
- particular lessons that only a malformed or diseased body would negotiate, so the disease or malformation is nourished until the lessons are learned;
- basic cause is one's belief system (built from this incarnation and from past incarnations); belief systems cause the emotional attitude one takes toward life activity and experiences, these emotions change body chemistry, and body chemistry causes imbalance in the physical body or mental behavioral patterns;

belief systems can cause a war between the soul-mind and conscious mind and this disagreement causes one to engage in health-destroying habits, and acquire judgments regarding dis-eases, which in turn weakens resistance in the body cells.

Most complimentary medical systems today agree that health is a state of wholeness and balance, governed by a universal life force. Illness results from imbalances in the body that block the flow of the life force; symptoms can be seen as the body's attempt to self heal. The disease ("dis-ease") process is the continuing biological activity or function marked by gradual changes that lead toward a particular result.

Hippocrates said that "...during an illness, there are key points where a physician can intercede to assist the patient to restore health." Diagnosis is used to determine what type of dis-ease a client might have and the current stage of the dis-ease process. Typically the diagnostic process includes many expensive and time-consuming tests to determine the condition of the client. In Western medicine, these tests are considered necessary to come up with a diagnosis and, from that diagnosis, a recommended course of treatment. As an inexpensive and rapid alternative, I offer the PRSM CHART, which includes the use of pendulum and charts to aid in the rapid identification of health problems.

Medical Dowsing as a Healing Tool

1. *Medical Dowsing* expands our awareness of diagnostic possibilities

According to *Funk & Wagnalls Standard Dictionary*, diagnosis is the "art or act of discriminating between diseases and of distinguishing them by their characteristic symptoms." When we make a diagnosis of a client's condition, we are relying on our own belief patterns which have been pre-established by both extensive training and experience. An issue can arise, however, if we identify a problem as the same problem we have dealt with many times before, then label it and choose a treatment method based upon that assumption without considering other options - basically having "tunnel vision."

The word *belief* is defined as "probable knowledge or a mental conviction; acceptance of something as true or actual." Beliefs are born in our subconscious mind as a result of conscious mind input, our cultural exposure to fears and attitudes, prior responses to actions and feedback, and judgments about the overall experience. Once we have set up these belief structures, we experience our lives in a way that confirms those adopted beliefs on the conscious level. Thus our beliefs can again lock us into a line of thinking - tunnel vision again - causing us to miss other possibilities.

By using these pendulum charts and our superconscious mind, we can bypass the old beliefs and be open to all possibilities.

2. *Medical Dowsing* **can save money**

Time and money are other key factors in making a health diagnosis. Diagnostic tests are often extremely expensive and the testing methods are not always definitive. The typical process of diagnostic elimination takes precious time for trial and error to rule out the many possible causes of a problem and pinpoint specific sources of trouble. By using PRSM dowsing, a person can quickly and effectively determine a potential diagnosis, and then choose more sophisticated diagnostic tests to either confirm or rule it out.

3. *Medical Dowsing* **helps us to understand the body level or levels involved in the dis-ease process**

The dis-ease process is a natural, progressively continuing development marked by a series of gradual changes that succeed one another in a relatively fixed way and leading toward a particular result or end. The dis-ease process can occur on any of our vibrational body levels, from the physical up to the mental body. It is commonly believed among complementary care practitioners that most dis-ease begins at the higher vibrational body levels. These dis-ease vibrations are dormant until triggered by an event causing symptoms to start manifesting on the physical level. For example, a person who complains of back pain that dowses as originating on an emotional level can receive physical treatment like chiropractic or massage and may experience temporary pain relief. However, that treatment does not effectively remove the emotional source. Within days, the emotional blocks can start rebuilding the problem in the physical body and the client ends up with back pain again.

A second possible health scenario is that a problem that tests on the emotional body level may not yet show up during a physical exam. If this energy is not addressed, the person will most likely see physical symptoms sometime in the future.

By understanding how different level(s) of dis-ease can manifest in a person, we can choose the best method to clear it and more effectively direct any healing efforts. For example, if a client is extremely fearful about the possibility of having cancer, cancer may dowse positive at his or her mental body level. The best treatment of choice would be some type of counseling support to alleviate those fears rather than a more aggressive physical approach. If the cancer is already testing on the physical level, both a physical approach to address the cancer and a mental change is needed for total healing.

4. *Medical Dowsing* **helps us to create a bridge between the physical and spiritual aspects of healing**

Another important factor in healing is that we are bonded to other souls on both the physical and spiritual planes. Our bodies are a collection of vibrational layers ranging from the seemingly very solid but slowly vibrating physical level to the limitless ONE, and can be affected by others (spouse, co-workers, family members, etc.) on the physical plane. On the spiritual level, our guardian angels, guides or other entities such as *discarnates* (ghosts) caught in our energy field may activate our 'dis-ease triggers.' By pendulum dowsing with the appropriate charts, we can be made aware of these other possibilities and address them.

5. *Medical Dowsing* helps to identify the message being sent by a dis-ease and to clear emotional blocks that prevent complete healing

According to information received through my High Self, less than 15% of our health problems actually originate in a current lifetime. The rest are reactions to past life patterns of dis-ease or trauma which make us susceptible to specific physical issues in this lifetime. Entities bonded to us, such as guardian angels or guides, can carry the same dis-ease patterns as we have and their proximity to us may then trigger or strengthen those patterns in us.

In order to become whole again, we must heal the separateness that dis-ease represents. A health symptom can be seen as the body's subconscious attempt to communicate with us. All too often, the Western approach is to either surgically remove a part or a whole of a conflicted area in our bodies, or to try to mask our symptoms with medication. This approach does not always work because the dis-ease pattern or trauma has not been healed. To facilitate healing we need to first acknowledge the received body communication, and then find a way to release it by connecting to the correct information levels.

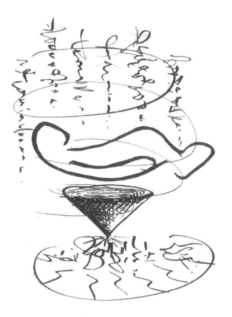

Figure 42 "LifeWeaving with PRSM"

CHAPTER 13

LifeWeaving and the PRSM Chart

The PRSM Chart

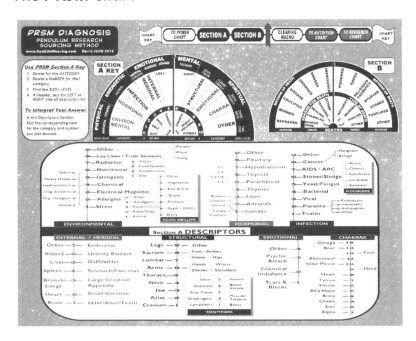

Figure 43 The PRSM Diagnostic Chart

For my acupuncture practice, long before **LifeWeaving** was developed, I created the Pendulum Research Sourcing Method (PRSM)

CHART as a means to find the underlying cause of dis-ease. PRSM includes two separate dowsing charts - *Section A Key* and *Descriptors* (the primary PRSM CHART), and *Section B* to learn more about past life deaths or injuries.

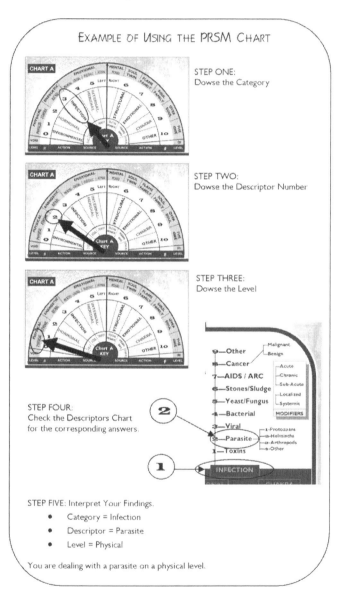

Figure 44 Simple Example of Using the PRSM CHART

PRSM Diagnosis Protocol

Begin by placing your pendulum into a neutral swing over the PRSM *Chart Key* neutral line and follow steps 1 – 9.

If directed to *Section A*, continue as described below:

1. Place your pendulum over the neutral line of the *Section A Key* and ask *"What category needs treatment at this time?"*

2. *"Which number in the category?"* (Check the *Descriptors Section* for the possible range. *E.g.,* the *Infection* category has nine options to choose from, the *Emotional* category has only four options.)

3. Ask *"Left or right side of the category listings?"* (Many of the categories have choices on both the left and right sides of the numbers so test to see which side to use for interpretation.)

4. Using the *Body Level* outer ring section on the *Section A Key*, ask *"What body level is the problem on?"*

5. Go to *Section A Descriptors* to interpret your results. You can also test *Identifiers, Food Groups, Modifiers* or sub-categories as needed. For example, if you want to know more about the specific nature of a structural problem, refer to **PRSM** *Section A Descriptors, Structural* section, *Identifiers* box. Use a number chart and then test for left or right side to find and interpret your answers.

6. Select a treatment method of choice or clear the issue using **LifeWeaving**.

7. After the clearing or treatment, recheck to see *"What body level does this clear to?"* (physical to the infinity range). If it stops at a new level, go through the clearing steps again, this time using the new level plus the original issue as your statement to clear.

   E.g., after treatment, the sacrum clears to 100% on the physical level yet in retesting, the pendulum stops at the mental level. You must now repeat the *Basic LifeWeaving Protocol* and clear using *"sacrum mental level"* for your statement. If you selected a different form of treatment, you now know that you should address both the client's mental state as well as the physical.

8. Retest and ask, *"Are there any contributing factors?"* Contributing factors can be directly or indirectly affecting a problem. (Using an example of sciatic pain, the testing might show *Structural #3*, left side on the *Buddhic* emotional level = left jaw on the emotional level. Since the sciatic nerve actually starts in the head, chronic jaw tension could be causing sciatic pain in the left hip and leg. This finding now gives us the jaw to also target for treatment.) Continue testing, identifying and clearing issues until the pendulum stays on neutral for contributing factors.

9. Retest asking *"Is there anything else we should ask about?"* This question allows the practitioner to discover other avenues needing research that might otherwise be missed, or to find a seemingly unrelated health issue that needs attention.

An Example of Working with the PRSM Chart

STEP 1 - Place your pendulum into a neutral swing over *Section A Key* neutral line.

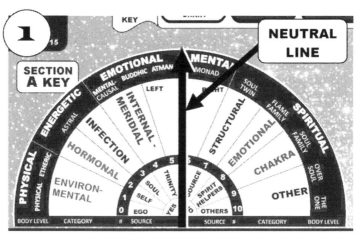

STEP 2 - Ask *"What category needs treatment at this time?"*

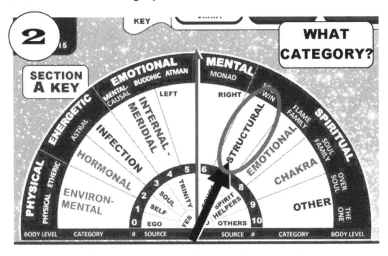

(The example shows "structural" category)

STEP 3 - *"Which number in the category?"* [Test using the available range of numbers by checking the *Descriptors chart* section. E.g., the *Structural* category has nine options to choose from.]

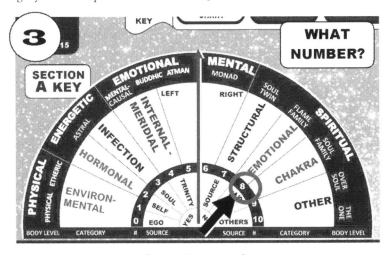

(Example shows #8)

STEP 4 - *"Left or right side of the category?"* [Many of the categories have choices on both left and right sides of the line so test to see which side to interpret.]

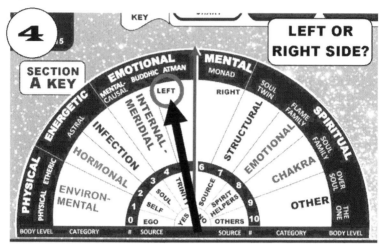

(Example tests 'left side')

STEP 5 - *"What body level is the problem on?"*

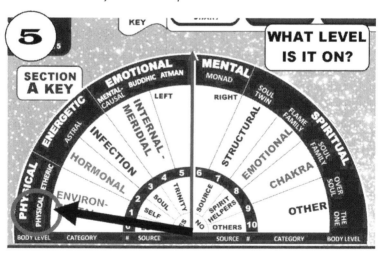

(Tests as physical level)

STEP 6 - Use *Descriptors Section A* to interpret your results.

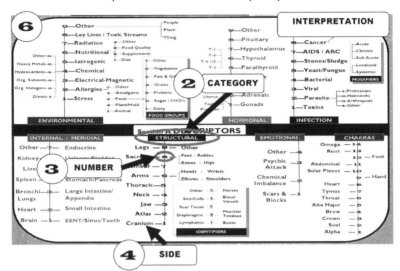

(Tests as Structural, #8, left side, physical level = sacrum on the physical level)

STEP 7 - Use *Identifiers, Food Groups, Modifiers* or subcategories as needed. [Test using a number and a left-right chart to find and interpret your answers.]

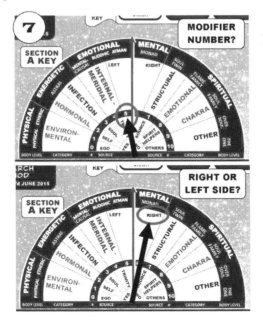

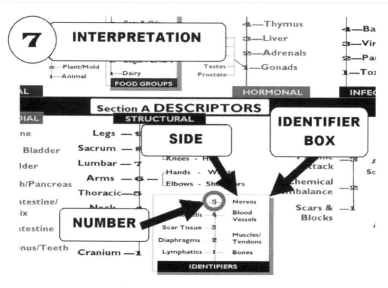

(Tests as #5, Right = nerves.)

STEP 8 - Select a treatment method of choice or take it to the POWER CHART and clear the issue using the *Basic LifeWeaving Protocol.*

STEP 9 - After clearing or treatment, recheck *"What body level does this issue clear to (from physical to spiritual range)?"*

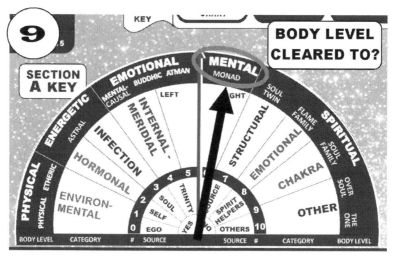

(Our example tests cleared to the *Mental* level)

*[Use the Basic LifeWeaving Protocol to clear 'the problem at this mental level'
until it tests as neutral with no blockages.]*

STEP 10 - Ask *"Are there any contributing factors?"* *[Continue testing
and clearing contributing factors until a neutral response is obtained]*

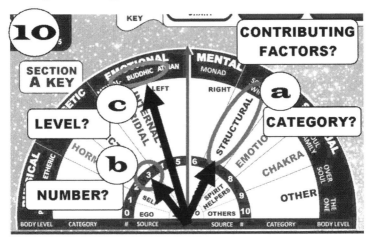

(Example tests as Structural, #3, Buddhic emotional level = jaw)

STEP 11 - Final Check. Once all contributing factors have been found
and cleared, retest and ask *"Is there anything else we should ask
about?"* *[This question allows the practitioner to find information important to the
case that might otherwise be missed. The client might also have a seemingly unrelated
health issue that needs attention.]*

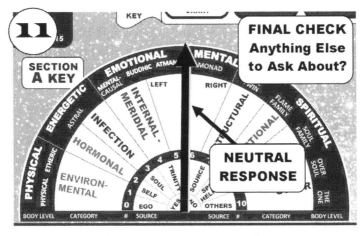

(Our example tests as neutral.)

Example Summary

In this example we have determined the following:

CHIEF COMPLAINT: Sacral pain

PRSM TESTING DIAGNOSIS: Structural, the sacrum on the physical level with nerve involvement. There is a secondary contributing factor of jaw tightness due to emotional issues.

PRESCRIPTION: Reduce nerve inflammation to reduce pain; reduce jaw tension by alleviating the emotional blockage.

TREATMENT: Can include any number of approaches including LifeWeaving, acupuncture, massage, etc., addressing both the jaw and tailbone.

CHAPTER 14

PRSM Section A: Key and Descriptors

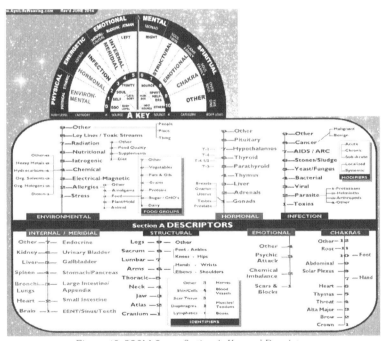

Figure 45 PRSM CHART *Section A: Key and Descriptors*

Source of Pendulum Information

The *Source of Information* section is used to ensure accurate dowsing by checking for the origin of your pendulum information.

This section lists possible sources that can affect answers during the dowsing:

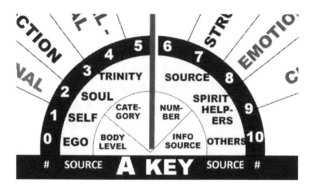

Figure 46 PRSM CHART *Section A: Yes-No, Numbers, Source of Information*

- **Ego** - represents a combination of the conscious and subconscious mind. The ego is established from all present and past life experiences, and from one's attitude toward those experiences, which makes the ego a very poor source for information.
- **Self** - according to Carl Jung, the self is an evolutionary unit emerging from nature, functioning to develop as a human being. The self is also a poor source of information.
- **Soul (High Self, Soul Committee)** - the invisible life force of existence found in every living thing. This is a good source for obtaining information during dowsing.
- ***Personal Trinity*** - the term used to indicate the harmonized Self, Soul and Ego. This *Trinity* aligned with the Divine Plan, gives the best overall answers for a person.
- **Source (God, the One)** - your most accurate answers come from connecting your harmonized *Personal Trinity* to the Divine Plan.
- **Spirit Helpers** - spirit helpers are assigned souls, guardian angels or guides working with a person. Information from this source cannot always be trusted. Demand that all answers come through the harmonized *Trinity/God* and then retest to confirm.
- **Others** - can either be incarnated (a spouse, a doubting associate or friend) or a spirit (good, bad or indifferent). Any information from this source is not to be trusted.

The best dowsing answers come from your harmonized *Personal Trinity* aligned with the Divine Plan.

PRSM Categories

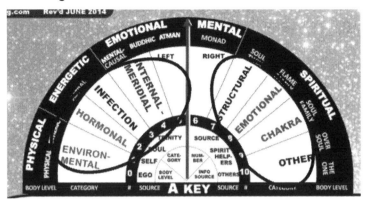

Figure 47   PRSM CHART *Section A Key: Categories*

If a PRSM *Categories* tests positive, the practitioner can try to clear the entire category without identifying any specifics (*e.g.,* simply clearing the entire *Hormonal* category vs. identifying a specific gland). However, sometimes the more specific you can get in your clearing work, the better. I find that starting with general clearing usually works fine. Feel free to test more specifically if there is little or no change following treatment.

The PRSM CHART *Descriptors* in each category are listed below and will be described in greater detail in the following chapters.

- **Environmental** - Stress, Allergies, Electrical and/or Magnetic, Chemical, Iatrogenic, Nutritional, Radiation, Ley Lines or Toxic Streams and other.
- **Hormonal** - Gonads, Adrenals, Liver, Thymus, Parathyroid, Thyroid, Hypothalamus, Pituitary and other.
- **Infection** - Toxins, Parasites, Virus, Bacteria, Yeast or Fungus, Stones or Sludge, AIDS or ARC (AIDS-Related Complex), Cancer and other.
- **Internal-Meridial** - Includes all the internal organs - Brain, EENT (Ears, Eyes, Nose and Throat)/Sinus/Teeth, Heart, Small

Intestine, Lungs or Bronchi, Large Intestine and Appendix, Spleen, Stomach and Pancreas, Liver, Gallbladder, Kidney, Urinary Bladder, and Endocrine System. This list also correlates to the paired acupuncture meridians.

- **Structural** - Bones, Muscles, Skin/Cells, Lymph, Nerves, Diaphragms, and Blood Vessels.
- **Emotional** - scars and blocks, chemical imbalance, and psychic attack.
- **Chakra** - all the regular Chakras as well as Hand and Foot, Alpha and Omega, Soul and Alta Major chakras.

Numbers and Left-Right

- **The Numbers** on this chart range from 0-10.
- **The Left-Right Categories** help identify a health issue when the descriptors list has answers on both left and right side.

Body Levels (Levels of Dis-Ease)

The *Body Level* section of the PRSM CHART can be used to determine which body levels are involved, or what level is blocked by a dis-ease or emotional issue.

- **Physical Body Level** (includes the Etheric pattern) - is comprised of chemicals assimilated in a living field that gives it shape. It has the lowest rate of vibration of all the bodies that comprise us. At this level, health problems materialize in the form of symptoms or discomfort significant enough to get our attention. This body level is associated with the earth element.
- **Etheric Body** (paired with the physical level) - an invisible electromagnetic field that surrounds and interpenetrates the physical body at a faster vibrational rate than the physical. The etheric body is affected by outside influences such as moon, tides, light and dark, and other environmental factors. This body serves as a pattern for future emotions and character traits, and is considered the seat of all memory. The etheric body also acts as a battery for the body's health and vitality by absorbing universal life force

through the chakra system. This vibrational body level stays with the physical body until it fully decays. This etheric body is associated with the air element.

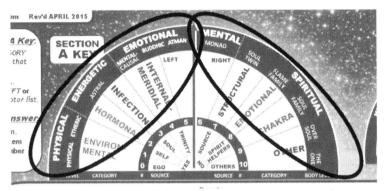

Figure 48 PRSM CHART Section A Key: Body Levels

- **Astral or Energetic Body** - includes two bodies, the lower and the higher astral, which extends five to eight inches outward from the physical body. The astral body level is affected by our physical existence, and acts as a link between the etheric level and the mental level by receiving and transmitting energy vibrations. The astral body holds the emotions of the physical in memory form only and has no conscious mind yet it is still subject to the Earth's desires and habits. The astral body is able to separate from the physical at will. At death, the astral body maintains information about emotional, mental, and etheric issues needed for future incarnations.

- **Emotional Body** - is directly linked to our emotions and the Feeling Nature of God, and is associated with the water element. This body includes the Lower Mental-Causal, Buddhic and Atman levels.

  o **Lower Mental Body** - interpenetrates the physical body at the hip line and extends upward and outward into the ether. This is where our intuitive or gut feelings form. This body level is also believed to control the cerebrospinal system. The causal body, also called the "intelligent body" or the "higher mental body," functions to analyze the lives of the soul-mind as presented by the mental body and acts as a storehouse for the essence of all experience gained through previous incarnations. The soul-mind, vibrating faster than the physical body, manages and directs the body; it helps to sustain and improve the physical body and lifestyle of the individual for the duration of the incarnation.

o **Buddhic Body** - interpenetrates and extends a large distance from the physical. It serves to connect to and motivates our causal level to such issues as universal love, spiritual awareness, discrimination, and humanitarian needs. The Buddhic level works with our Soul (High Self) as intuitional information and inspirational thoughts.

o **Atman Body** - interpenetrates and extends a large distance from the physical. After the other bodies are discarded, the Atman body acts as a strainer, separating the waste of unnecessary reactions from karma now overcome. The waste is dissolved so the soul-mind is purified.

- **Mental or Monad Body** - considered to be the indestructible unit of our existence - a concentrated mass of energy and intelligence containing a complete replica of when it was in its original perfect state. C.W. Leadbeater calls it the "life-wave of divine force." It is the divine spark of God in every living thing that remembers when God was One. The monadic plane of soul consciousness is a place where Totality's plan begins and ends. From this plane, a spark from Totality radiates from itself and projects into the planes below creating more and more characteristics. Each of these sparks creates a soul-mind which radiates to denser vibrations. The soul-mind wants to return to Totality, but it must learn what needs to be learned from the lower planes before it can do so. At this monad level, a living mirror of the universe, we are closed off from one another, but sensitive to the vibrations of the universe. Patricia Cota-Robles considers the mental body as separate from the physical brain structure but acting as the vehicle through which our creative faculties of thought are expressed. This body is linked to the Realms of Thought and the Divine Mind of God. The mental body is associated with the fire element.

- **Spiritual Bodies**
  - o **Soul Twin or Exact Soul Mate** - the result of two monads splitting from one monadic entity to go through evolvement. They are individualistic as well as complementary beings.
  - o **Flame Family** - usually includes nine souls or monads that split into duality (soul twins). These eighteen souls spend lifetimes closely interacting with each other in a variety of relationships, lessons and experiences.
  - o **Soul Family** - consists of a large group of souls connected by a common purpose. The soul family is like a flower with many petals (flame families), each group working on their part of the whole purpose.
  - o **Oversoul** - the part of the soul-mind that separates and stores all the activities a soul has experienced in Earthly incarnations that were handled with the correct attitude.
  - o **The One or Divine Body, Source** - the Macrocosm, the Un-Manifested Interdependent Intelligence, the Totality, the Godhead; consisting of all vibrational frequencies that will ever exist, that mankind will ever comprehend, and that mankind will ever find necessary to use.

Descriptors Chart

The *Descriptors Section* expands the seven categories found on PRSM *Section A Key* by listing category and subcategory elements for further testing. Those elements are numbered so by dowsing the *Section A Key* for category and then a number (and occasionally left or right), the practitioner can go to the corresponding category and number on the *Descriptors Chart* for answers.

Subcategories, Modifiers and Identifiers

When using the PRSM CHART, you can test subsections of various categories, such as the *Identifiers Chart* associated with the *Structural Descriptors* and identify the exact type of tissue involved - nerves, muscles, bones, etc. Or you can test the best treatment

Figure 49 PRSM Chart *Section A: Descriptors*

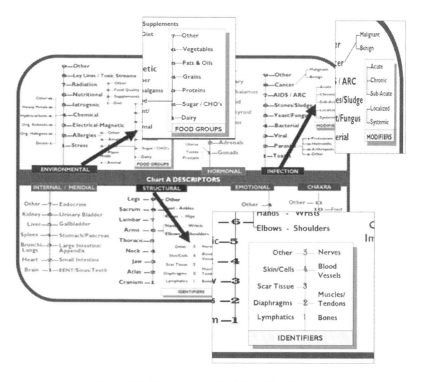

Figure 50 Subcategories, Modifiers, Identifiers

approach for thyroid, or pick out a specific food group. However, I recommend that you only test far enough to complete the clearing or select your treatment methods.

When using the PRSM CHART, you can test subsections of various categories, such as the *Identifiers Chart* associated with the *Structural Descriptors* and identify the exact type of tissue involved - nerves, muscles, bones, etc. Or you can test the best treatment approach for thyroid, or pick out a specific food group. However, I recommend that you only test far enough to complete the clearing or select your treatment methods.

In the following chapters, each element in the various *Descriptor Sections* will be presented in greater detail. This includes information from both Western and Chinese medicine, as well as energetic, emotional and metaphysical links and definitions.

CHAPTER 15

PRSM Section A: Environmental Factors

Introduction

Environmental Factors, any of which can affect us negatively, range from forces of nature like underground streams, to man-made forces like electricity. Environmental factors also include chemicals, allergens or even other people who can have affect on our.

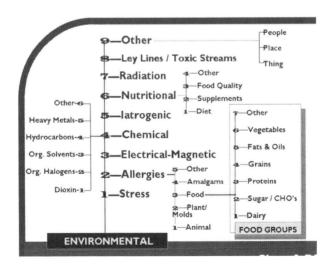

Figure 51 PRSM CHART *Descriptors: Environmental Factors*

Definitions, discussions and further testing suggestions for this environmental category are listed below.

Environmental Descriptors

#1— Stress

- **Definition:** Stress is any combination of forces exerting undue pressure or distress on a person.
- **Discussion:** Stress includes all general stress conditions such as work environment and job pressures, relationships, life conditions, etc. Hans Selye, an expert in stress research, concluded that "it is not the stressors that create health problems but rather our reaction to them."

#2— Allergies

- **Definition:** (1) hypersensitivity to an antigen in response to a first exposure; (2) exaggerated or pathological reaction (sneezing, respiratory, itching, or skin rashes) to substances, situations, or physical states that are without comparable effect on the average individual.

Note that food sensitivities can change depending on a person's overall state of health, stress, eating habits, etc.

Subcategories:

1) Animal
2) Plants/Molds
3) Food (Also test for which food group):
    - Diary
    - Sugar / CHO's (carbohydrates)
    - Proteins
    - Grains
    - Fats & Oils
    - Vegetables
    - Other
4) Amalgams (mercury-silver dental fillings)
5) Other

- **Further Testing**: If the client tests positive for allergies, dowse to identify the specific category. Also, you can quickly identify allergens in a specific category as follows:

Rapid Allergy Testing Protocol

1. Place your pendulum into a neutral swing along any neutral line on the chart.
2. Add in the client's harmonized *Personal Trinity* (the pendulum should remain in its neutral swing).
3. Mentally or verbally add in the food you want to test.
4. If the client is compatible with a substance, the pendulum will remain on neutral. If the client is allergic to a substance, the pendulum will move to the left of the neutral line which also roughly indicates the degree of sensitivity. So in addition to checking for allergies, ask "*What % harm?*" and "*What % compatibility?*" for the client to use the substance.

   Note: If the pendulum moves to the right of the neutral line, the positive allergy response is likely due to one or more of the client's spirit guides or guardian angels. Be sure that any spirit helpers with sensitivities are all either cleared or removed by saying "*Educate, elevate, remove or replace any spirits with issues with this substance.*"
5. Try clearing any positives using the *Basic LifeWeaving Protocol* and then retest the client for the same allergen.

Note: You can test different brands, different types of products, organic vs. inorganic, etc. in order to find the most compatible variety of a food for a client.

For example, if dairy tests positive, put your pendulum and the client's harmonized *Personal Trinity* on the neutral line and mentally add in different types of milk (whole, low-fat, fat-free, cow's, soy, rice, almond, coconut, goat's, etc.). If the pendulum moves off the neutral line, there is a disharmony with a specific type of milk creating an allergy.

Likewise, if cheese allergy tests, add in various types of cheese (parmesan, cheddar, gouda, goat, Swiss, muenster, cottage, etc.) and watch for any imbalance (where the pendulum moves off the neutral line). If you often deal with allergy patients, you can make up your own pendulum testing charts to speed up this process.

#3—Electrical-Magnetic

- **Definition:** A magnetic field is created in the region of a magnet or current-carrying body. Electromagnetism is magnetism developed by electricity.

- **Discussion:** This category can test positive for people living or working around high tension wires or electronic equipment like computers, or if they continuously carry a cell phone on their person, or wear a Bluetooth ear piece.

- **Further Testing:** If you need to target exactly what is causing this type of environmental pollution, pendulum further by asking *"Is the problem electrical, magnetic or electromagnetic in nature?"* The best treatment is to remove the source generating the field.

#4—Chemical

- **Definition:** A chemical is a substance made by, used in, or produced by chemistry or the phenomenon of chemical reactions. The five major categories of chemicals are:

  1) **Dioxin** - a hormone-disrupting chemical formed as a by-product of the manufacture, molding, or burning of organic chemicals and plastics that contain chlorine. It is the most toxic man-made organic chemical, second only to radioactive waste.

  2) **Organic Halogens** - a large class of natural and synthetic chemicals that contain one or more halogens (fluorine,

chlorine, bromine, or iodine) combined with carbon and other elements.

3) **Organic Solvents** - are components of a solution that act as dissolving agents. The most familiar and widely used solvent is water. Other solvent compounds are acetone, alcohol, benzene, carbon disulfide, carbon tetra-chloride, chloroform, ether, ethyl acetate, furfural, gasoline, toluene, turpentine, and xylene or xylol.

4) **Hydrocarbons** - are any of a class of organic compounds composed only of carbon and hydrogen. These include many common natural substances such as natural gas, petroleum, asphalt, or are included in complex mixtures.

5) **Heavy Metals** - loosely defined in medical usage, include all toxic metals regardless of their atomic weight. While humans require some heavy metals such as iron, cobalt, copper, manganese, molybdenum and zinc, excessive levels can be harmful. Other heavy metals such as mercury, plutonium, and lead are toxic metals that have no known vital or beneficial effect on organisms and, over time, their accumulation in the body can cause serious illness.

- **Discussion:** The chemical section may test positive if the client has a history of exposure to chemical pollutants - either from past exposure or if they currently work with chemicals (mechanics, gasoline attendants, painters, etc.).

#5—Iatrogenic

- **Definition:** Iatrogenic literally means "pertaining to being created by the physician."
- **Discussion:** These are medically-induced problems (often side effects) from a treatment, a drug or supplement given by a Western medical or alternative healthcare provider, or even a client who self-medicates incorrectly.

#6—Nutritional

- **Definition:** the organic process of nourishing or being nourished; the processes by which an organism assimilates food and uses it for growth and maintenance.
- **Subcategories:**
  - **Diet** - is what and how the client is eating *("Fast food?" " Vegetarian or vegan?" "On a diet?" "How many meals a day?" "Balanced meals?")*.
  - **Supplements** - are what the client is taking beyond food to make up for deficiencies *("Vitamins?" "Minerals?" "Amino acids?" "Oils?" "Probiotics?")*.
  - **Food Quality** - how food has been grown *("Organic?" "Inorganic?")*, handled *("Processed?" "Fresh?" "Frozen" "Canned?")* and prepared *("Raw?" "Baked?" "Broiled?" "Grilled?" "Microwaved?")*.
  - **Other** - *"Cravings?" "Dislikes?"*.
- **Discussion:** If the nutritional category tests positive, find the positive subcategory and explore further.

#7—Radiation

- **Definition:** The act of radiating or the state of being radiated.
- **Discussion:** This section may test positive for persons undergoing radiation therapy or being exposed to some other source of radiation - either man-made (isotopes, x-rays, etc.) or natural (radon gas given off by granite, etc.).

#8—Ley Lines/Toxic Streams

- **Definition:** The *ley lines* are the latitude and longitude lines of the electromagnetic net covering the Earth. This category includes the Becker-Hagens Grid Map, Black Lines, Curry Lines, Hartmann Net or Hartmann Lines, Ley Lines, and Schumann Waves/Resonance.

Toxic streams are underground streams containing high concentrations of minerals that can produce an energy field strong enough to disturb the health of a person living above it.

- **Discussion:** Where the various energy lines intersect, a very small but intense electromagnetic (EM) force is produced. If this intersection point occurs exactly where a person sleeps, the person's health can be affected in subtle ways (insomnia, restlessness, headaches, unexplained aches and pains), or not so subtle ways (cancer). In sensitive people, toxic streams can produce the same types of health problems as ley lines.

#9—Other (People . . . Place . . . Thing)

- **Definition:** This category includes anything not already mentioned.
- **Discussion:** You can pendulum whether *"An issue is due to a person, place or thing?"* Then continue to research until the problem area is further identified and finally cleared.

CHAPTER 16

PRSM Section A: Hormonal Factors

Introduction

Hormones, produced by the endocrine glands, are transported through the body via blood and lymphatic systems. This glandular system is thought to energize, recharge and circulate energy in the body, much like an electrical generator. The hormones produced can affect either the entire body or a particular organ. In his book *The Complete System of Self-Healing Internal Exercises*, author Stephen Chang describes the hormonal system as "...vessels that are attached to one another by a series of arteries or tubes. Each vessel (gland) is dependent upon all others for its supply of liquid (energy)." As a result, if one gland is low, then all will readjust by dropping to a lower level.

Figure 52   A Balanced But Low Endocrine System

On a metaphysical level, the hormonal system represents the integration and balance of a person's entire life, including any attitudes and responses. The endocrine system also connects to the chakra system and universal energy.

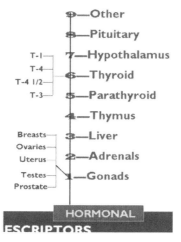

Figure 53 PRSM CHART *Section A Descriptors: Hormonal*

Hormonal Descriptors:

#1— Gonads

- **Definition:** Include the prostate and testes in men; and the vagina, uterus, ovaries and breasts in women.
- **Function:** Responsible for hormone production, sexual energy, sexual response and reproduction. The gonads produce and lend energy or "fire" to the rest of the glands.
- **Discussion:** Chinese medical pathology recognizes that gonads can be damaged by either too much use ("affairs of the bedroom") or too little if the sexual energy has no outlet, either through sex or creative endeavors that transform and utilize the energy.
- **Emotions:** The gonads reflect our ability to give and to receive pleasure, greed, selfishness, deception, feeling unproductive, or anger towards a partner.

#2— Adrenals

- **Location:** On top of the kidneys.
- **Function:** Support kidney, bone, bone marrow and spine function. These glands produce adrenaline, a form of epinephrine, which increases respiration, heart rate and energy. They

also affect protein metabolism, mineral balance, immune response, bone health and sex hormones. These hormones also have an anti-inflammatory property.

- **Emotions:** Anxiety and no longer caring for yourself.

#3— Liver

- **Location:** In the right upper abdomen.
- **Function:** Creates, regulates and stores some of the hormones in the body in addition to almost 1000 other body functions, including detoxification.
- **Emotions:** Anger and constriction of emotions and energy.

#4— Thymus

- **Location:** Close above the heart.
- **Function:** Governs both the heart and circulatory system. Western science also recognizes that the thymus produces T-lymphocytes which mobilize to attack and destroy foreign cells in the body, thus making the thymus an important part of our immune system.
- **Discussion:** In Chinese medicine the thymus is referred to as the "House of the Heart." It is essential for a healthy immune system and, if positive, indicates a more advanced problem.
- **Emotions:** Feeling attacked by life.

#5— Parathyroid

- **Location:** Behind the thyroid gland in the neck.
- **Function:** Helps to regulate calcium uptake or loss by the body.
- **Discussion:** A malfunctioning parathyroid may be an underlying cause of osteoporosis. Even though a person takes enough calcium, if this gland is malfunctioning his or her body may not be able to absorb calcium correctly, so it is excreted.
- **Emotions:** Tired all the time, depression, doesn't feel well; feels old, can't concentrate, sleeps poorly, and irritable.

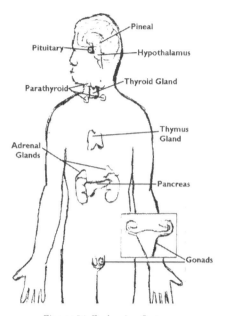

Figure 54 Endocrine System

#6— Thyroid

- **Location:** Just below the larynx in the throat.
- **Function:** Regulates metabolism of cells in the body, thus governing growth as well as water retention. The thyroid is also associated with the respiratory system in Chinese medicine. Since treatment varies according to the particular malfunction in the gland, the following sub-categories, identified by D. A. Versandaal, D.C., can be used for determining the best treatment approach.
- **Sub-categories:**
  - o **T– 1** - Controls/electrifies the brain. Symptoms include crabbiness, paranoia, having fear/anxiety, and being mentally fatigued. One alternative treatment available from Standard Process Laboratories (SP) is Mintran, a formula made from kelp, seaweed and minerals.
  - o **T-3** - Triiodothyronine governs the kidneys. Symptoms include "lazy kidneys," edema, loose bowels (colitis, diverticulitis, Crohn's Disease). An alternative treatment available

from Standard Process Laboratories is a combination of Thytrophin PMG plus Hepatrophin to help the liver process this hormone from T-4.

o **T-4** - Thyroxin, the primary hormone produced by the thyroid gland, delivers energy to the cells. A deficiency causes symptoms including a lot of coughing when older, chronic fatigue, depression, or headaches; needing frequent cervical adjustments because treatments do not hold well. An alternative treatment for low T4 is Thytrophin PMG, a complete   thyroid supplementation product from SP.

o **"T-41/2"** - The primary symptom of a "T-4$^{1/2}$" thyroid is depression. It is differentiated from a T-4 problem, which requires full thyroid supplementation, because it simply requires iodine for treatment. Standard Process offers Prolamine Iodine as one choice.

Note: Standard Process products can be ordered through licensed practitioners such as chiropractors, acupuncturists, and some medical doctors. For more information visit the SP website at www.standardprocess.com or contact me at www.AyniLifeWeaving.com.

▪ **Emotions:** Humiliation or anger with God.

#7— Hypothalamus

▪ **Location:** Just above the brain stem, under the thalamus. This organ is a portion of the 3rd ventricle of the brain.

▪ **Function:** The hypothalamus acts as the principle intermediary between the nervous system and the endocrine system. This gland stimulates or inhibits the pituitary as needed to balance out the regulation of carbohydrates, fats, proteins, some ions and some sexual function. It also controls the autonomic nervous system which regulates the internal organs, helps receive sensory input, and controls hunger, thirst, rage, aggression, sleep and awake states. The hypothalamus helps form the limbic system, the intermediate part of the brain that houses emotions.

- **Emotions:** Survival issues.

#8— Pituitary

- **Location:** Sits at the base of the brain close to the hypothalamus.
- **Function:** Known as the "master gland," the pituitary regulates the activities of the other endocrine glands. It is involved in overall growth and development, milk production in pregnant women, regulates adrenals, thyroid and sex organs, skin pigmentation, water metabolism and uterine contraction during childbirth. Chinese medicine views this gland as governing memory, wisdom, intelligence and thought.
- **Emotions:** Entitlement issues.

#9— Other

Other hormone producers in the body include:

- **Kidneys** - help to degrade insulin in the body and produce both prostaglandins, the unsaturated fatty acid hormones present in many tissues of the body, as well as rennin, which helps to regulate blood pressure.
- **Pancreas** - regulates blood sugar with secretions of insulin and glucagon.
- **Pineal gland** - secretes serotonin as well as melatonin, affecting the ovaries.
- **Intestines** - secrete the hormone cholecystokinin that stimulates secretion of bile and digestive juices from the pancreas. Intestines also make secretin, which stimulates production of a bicarbonate-rich fluid by the pancreas and liver.

CHAPTER 17

PRSM Section A: Infection Factors

Introduction

Infection is defined as the act of infecting, as with dis-ease, attitude, mood, or ideas. It is the establishment of a pathogen in the host it has invaded. The factors found in the infection section of the PRSM CHART *Section A Descriptors* can refer to actual physical level infections (yeast, bacterial or viral), to toxins produced by an infecting agent (staphylococcus food poisoning or botulism, etc.), or to emotional levels represented by an infective agent (bacteria is "small bits of anger" or a virus can be "tiny bits of anger"). Cancer and AIDS have been addressed separately.

If any serious infection factor comes up consistently in testing, the client should be advised to have a Western medical checkup. However, it is common to see an infection issue test on an energetic level (astral, emotional or mental), and then clear as the client's emotional attitude changes.

Infection Descriptors

#1— Toxins

- **Definition:** A poisonous material that includes any type of residual poisons, whether from bacterial infection, animals or chemicals.
- **Location:** Liver, lymphatic system or any part of the body.

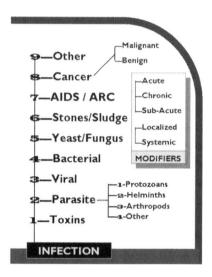

Figure 55 PRSM CHART *Section A Descriptors: Infection*

#2— Parasites

- **Definition:** Animals or plants that live on or in another organism obtaining nourishment at the other's expense. They keep the host alive while continually draining them of nourishment, stressing the immune system and preventing complete healing from happening.

  There are three general classifications of human parasites:

  1) **Protozoa** - One-celled organisms such as Giardia, E.coli, E. hystolytica, etc. The basic protozoan sub-groups are flagellates, amoeboids, sporozoans, and ciliates.

  2) **Helminths** - Various types of parasitic worms like tapeworms or hookworms. Sub-categories are cestodes, nematodes, and trematodes.

  3) **Arthropods** - Invertebrate animals that have an exoskeleton and a segmented body to which jointed appendages are

articulated in pairs. Some of the parasitic arthropods include ticks, scabies, lice, fleas and mites. Sub-groups include Crustacea, Insecta, and Chelicerata.

4) **Other** - Any other possibility not on the chart.

- **Location**: Any part of the body.
- **Discussion**: Parasites are common in man and are difficult and expensive to detect with lab testing. It is helpful to ask your client for details of travel to any country known as a common source of parasites. Also be aware that the subconscious mind sometimes registers other humans as parasites (feeding off you, yet not enough to kill you).
- **Symptoms**: Symptoms of parasites can range from diarrhea to constipation, general fatigue, weight gain, inability to lose weight, and bloating.
- **Further Testing**: Research *"where and on what body level is the parasite infecting?" "localized or systemic?" "chronic or acute?"*
- **Emotions**: Giving power to others; letting them take over.

#3— Viral

- **Definition**: Tiny pathogenic (disease-producing) agents capable of transmitting specific dis-eases.
- **Discussion**: A positive pendulum test for virus can represent either the infective organism or sometimes tiny bits of anger.
- **Further Testing**: *"Is it an infective organism or an emotional problem?" "Is it chronic or acute?" "What body level is it on?" "Where is it located?"*
- **Emotions**: Lack of joy flowing through life; bitterness; tiny bits of anger.

#4— Bacterial

- **Definition**: Small microorganisms that can range from harmless and beneficial to virulent and lethal. Bacteria are classified as gram positive, gram negative; aerobic or anerobic.

- **Further Testing**: *'Is it the infective organism or an emotional problem?" " Is it chronic or acute?" 'What body level is it on?' 'Systemic or localized?" 'Where is it located?"*
- **Emotions**: Irritation, annoyance and small bits of anger.

#5— Yeast / Fungus

- **Definition**: Fungus, literally "mushroom," refers to macroscopic structures and morphology of some mushrooms and molds. Yeast is unicellular fungi.
- **Discussion**: Chronic yeast infections, like candidiasis, are fairly common following antibiotic treatment because normal gut flora is the first to be killed off by the drug. In a healthy person it is the sheer numbers of normal intestinal flora that keep the resident candida in check. Recurring yeast infections are also common since, between acute phases, yeast survives in areas of the body like the gallbladder or sinuses that have a poor blood supply. Later the infection can resurface and spread if the immune system becomes compromised.
- **Further Testing**: *'Is it the infective organism or an emotional problem?" 'Is it chronic or acute?" 'What body level is it on?" 'Systemic or localized?" 'Where is it located?"*
- **Emotions**: Denying your own needs. Not supporting yourself; being scattered.

#6— Stones / Sludge

- **Definition**: Mineral or cholesterol stones that affect either the kidney or the gallbladder.
- **Discussion**: Sludge, a common problem, is sand-like granules which totally or partially clog the thin ducts leading from the kidney or gallbladder. Sludge usually does not show up on an ultrasound exam, but can definitely be the cause of pain and discomfort. Stones are larger particles. Stones or sludge in the gallbladder or bile duct cause symptoms such as excessive gas,

bloating, discomfort behind the right shoulder blade, and/or abdominal pain.

- **Further Testing:** *"Is it stones or sludge?" "An emotional problem?" "Is it chronic or acute?" "What body level is it on?" "Where is it located?"*
- **Emotions:** Bitterness; hard thoughts; condemning; pride.

#7— AIDS (Acquired Immune Deficiency Syndrome) or ARC (Aids Related Complex)

- **Definition:** *AIDS* is caused by an HIV (human immunodeficiency virus) infection. The virus kills or damages cells of the body's immune system resulting in a variety of symptoms including depression, diarrhea, thrush, weight loss, nausea and vomiting, burning/tingling feet, lactic acidosis, sinus infection, fatigue, and lipodystrophy.

  ARC manifests in AIDS patients who have not yet developed major deficient immune function. *ARC* is characterized by fever with generalized lymphadenopathy, diarrhea, weight loss, minor opportunistic infections, and cytopenias (low blood counts).

- **Further Testing:** If you test this category, check the PRSM *Chart Key* to determine *"What body level it is it found on?"* ARC commonly shows up only on higher body levels (energetic, emotional or mental). Determine if it is *"An infective agent or an emotional problem?" "Is it chronic or acute?" "Where is it located?"*
- **Emotions:** Feeling defenseless and hopeless; nobody cares; strong belief in not being good enough.

#8— Cancer

- **Definition:** A class of dis-eases where a group of cells displays uncontrolled growth, sometimes spreading to other body locations. These are considered *malignant*. Tumors that are self-limiting are considered *benign*.
- **Discussion:** Be sure to identify if *benign* or *malignant* and what body level a cancer is found on because it can dowse as

positive even if on a non-physical level. Note that the term "cancer" is an emotionally loaded word so make sure your client understands the cancer is only testing on an energetic, emotional or mental level, and not on the physical.

- **Further Testing:** *'Is it malignant, benign, or both?'* *'Systemic or localized?'* Test with **PRSM** CHART *Section A Key* for *'What body level or levels it is on?'* and to identify its *'Location in the body?'* Since cancer has a range of causes from chemical to viral to emotional, you can also test for *'Its cause?'* Recommend that a client see his or her physician for Western testing, especially if the cancer tests as being on the physical body level or if an energetic, emotional or mental body level dowsing positive does not clear following treatment.

- **Emotions:** The expression of deep hurt; longstanding resentment; deep secret or grief eating away at the self; carrying hatreds.

#9— Other

- **Definition:** Any other thing which the body considers an outside invasion which is not listed on the chart. These can include attitudes, moods, ideas, etc.

Infection Modifiers

The *Infection Modifiers* section helps to further identify characteristics of an infection, allowing you to adjust your treatment approach to best address that particular problem level.

Clinical levels of infection

- **Acute** - having a recent onset and coming to a crisis quickly.
- **Chronic** - continuing over a long period.
- **Subacute** - between the acute and chronic phases. Infection at this stage is often hidden.

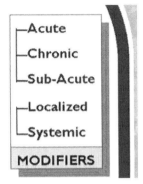

Figure 56 PRSM CHART *Section A Descriptors: Infection Modifiers*

Location/invasiveness of an infective agent can be:

- Systemic - spread over a wide area of the body.
- Localized - limited to a small area of the body.

CHAPTER 18

PRSM Section A: Internal/Meridial Factors

Introduction

The *Internal/Meridial* factors category corresponds to the actual organ's structure, function, and nerve enervation or to the corresponding acupuncture meridial pathway system. Ask *"Is a problem on the organ, meridial, or both levels?"* When a problem is found in an organ, obtain a baseline for both its structure (the way it is put together) and its function (normal physiological activity) in order to ascertain where the problem resides and to follow treatment changes and progress.

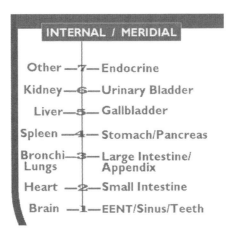

Figure 57 PRSM CHART *Section A Descriptors: Internal/Meridial*

Internal/Meridial Descriptors

#1 Left— Brain

- **Location:** In the skull and spinal column.
- **Further Testing:** Problems with the brain can be trauma-related like concussion, or chemically-related as in the case of depression or insomnia.
- **Emotions:** The brain represents the computer or switchboard of the body.
- **Chinese Medicine:** Called the "Sea of Marrow," the brain is responsible for the fluidity of movement in the body and for the sensitivity of the eyes and ears.

#1 Right— EENT (Ears, Eyes, Nose, Throat) /Sinus/Teeth) - Use your pendulum to identify which of these is the problem.

- **Location:** Face and throat.
- **Discussion on Teeth:** The teeth can harbor a hidden infection, which can be detrimental to the entire immune system of the body. Also, the teeth are a reflexology system and affect the entire body and are, in turn, affected by the body. Amalgam fillings, crowns and dental surgery can also cause the body to react.
- **Further Testing:** *'Which sense organ?' 'Right, left or both?' 'Functional, structural or both?'* Also check the emotional level with other questions such as *"What is it you don't want to hear?"* (if a patient has hearing problems), or *"What is it you don't want to see?"* (if the problem is with his or her eyesight).
- **Emotions:** Relate to our connection to the outside world. Throat and sinus problems often result from anger not spoken or from irritation to someone close to us (which may include ourselves).

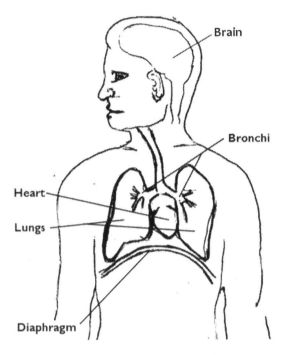

Figure 58 Organs of the Head and Chest

- Chinese Medicine:
  - o **Ears** - Kidneys open to the ears; the Triple Burner and Gallbladder acupuncture meridians pass through the ears and control them.
  - o **Eyes** - The liver opens to the eyes. Eyes reflect the state of all the organs because their pure *jing qi* (the *essence* received from one's parents at conception) pours through the eyes.
  - o **Nose** -The lungs open to the nose; the Stomach and Large Intestine meridians pass through the nose and control it.
  - o **Throat** -This is the "Door of the Lungs" but all organs are connected to the throat.
  - o **Teeth** -These are considered to be the "Excess of the Bone;" they are closely connected to the kidneys, which rule the bones.

#2 Left— Heart

- **Location**: Slightly left of the center of the chest.
- **Function**: The pump that regulates the flow of blood throughout the body.
- **Further Testing**: Ask *'Is the problem with the organ itself?" 'The meridians?" 'Blood pressure (BP)?" 'Anemia?"* (*"Due to deficient qi or of blood?'*). In anemia, find out through pendulum testing if it is *'Systemic or localized?"* And, if it is localized, *'In which organ or organs?"* You can also test for problems in each specific part of the heart including valves, muscle walls, the various chambers or nerve enervation.
- **Emotions**: Our ability for nurturing, unconditional love, compassion and forgiveness. Blocks to the flow of energy through the heart originate from emotions of hate, fear, and resentment.
- **Chinese Medicine**: The heart rules the blood and the blood vessels; it stores the *shen* (spirit); opens to the tongue. It is paired with the small intestine and associated with the element=fire, season=summer, color=red, emotion=joy, sound=laughing, taste=bitter.

#2 Right— Small Intestine

- **Location**: Center of the abdomen.
- **Function**: Literally, the small intestine separates what we eat and drink into what is nutritious and needs to be reabsorbed from what is waste matter and needs to move on into the colon for disposal.
- **Discussion**: The first portion of the small intestine, the duodenum, links the stomach to the jejunum and ileum. Both the bile and pancreatic ducts empty into this section.
- **Further Testing**: *'What portion is involved?" 'Is it a structural or functional problem or both?" 'What body level is it on?"*
- **Chinese Medicine**: The small intestine rules the separation of the pure (useful nutrients) from the turbid (the waste). It is paired with the heart and associated with the element=

fire, the season=summer, color=red, emotion=joy, sound= laughing, and taste=bitter.

#3 Left— Bronchi & Lungs

- **Location**: Chest.
- **Function**: Provide for the exchange of oxygen and carbon dioxide in the red cells through the walls of the alveoli.
- **Further Testing**: *"Lungs, bronchi or both?" "Left, right or both?" "Structure, function or both?" "Alveoli structure, function or both?"*
- **Emotions**: Grief or suffocation, and with our ability to receive love and show our openness and spontaneity. Along with grief, the lungs and bronchi reflect emotional suppression, relationship stress, resentment and anger, or too much stress and anxiety.
- **Chinese Medicine**: Lungs rule *qi*, move and adjust the water channels; rule the exterior of the body; open to the nose. Lungs are paired with the large intestine, and are associated with the element=metal, season=fall, color=white, emotion= grief, sound=weeping, taste=pungent.

#3 Right— Large Intestine & Appendix

- **Location**: The large intestine is found in the outlying areas of the lower abdomen. The appendix is located in the right lower abdomen.
- **Discussion**: The large intestine is comprised of four major sections: The cecum (the pouch where the small intestine joins the ascending colon), colon (ascending, transverse and descending segments), rectum, and anal canal.
- **Function**: Waste disposal.
- **Further Testing**: *"What portion is involved?" "Is it a structural or functional problem?" "What body level is it on?"*
- **Emotions**: Our ability to get rid of the waste in our lives.
- **Chinese Medicine**: The large intestine moves the turbid parts of food and fluids downward. The Large Intestine

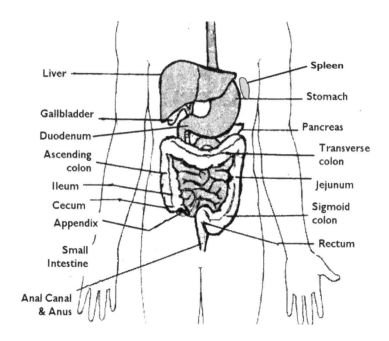

Figure 59 Internal Organs of the Abdomen

and Lung meridians are paired and associated with the ele-
ment=metal, season=fall, color=white or gray, emotion=grief,
sound=weeping, taste=pungent.

#4 Left— Spleen

- **Location:** Left upper abdomen.

- **Function:** The spleen a major organ of our immune system,
  is responsible for the final destruction of red blood
  cells, filtration and storage of blood, and production of
  lymphocytes.

- **Discussion:** Western medicine believes the spleen is "expend-
  able" since the liver and lymphatic system can take up much
  of the spleen's vital function. Chinese medicine describes the
  spleen as having a natural upward energy that helps to hold
  organs in place. If the spleen becomes weak, a person will
  start having problems with prolapsed organs (hemorrhoids,
  prolapsed uterus, etc.). The spleen is harmed by dampness in

the environment or by overly cold damp foods (like ice cream). If the spleen is weak, more problems of dampness such as phlegm, show up in the body.

- **Emotions:** Obsession.
- **Chinese Medicine:** The spleen rules transformation and transportation as the primary organ of digestion. It is paired with the stomach and associated with the element=earth, season=summer, color=yellow, emotion=pensiveness, sound= singing, taste=sweet.

#4 Right— Stomach/Pancreas

- **Location:** Left upper and middle abdomen.
- **Function:** The stomach digests and assimilates food. The pancreas produces digestive enzymes as well as insulin to help regulate sugar metabolism.
- **Discussion:** The stomach has a downward energy counter-balancing the spleen's natural upward movement. If the spleen is strong while the stomach is weak, nausea and vomiting can occur. If the spleen is weak and the stomach energy is very strong, diarrhea or organ prolapse can occur.
- **Further Testing:** *"Is is one organ or both?" "Function, structure or both?" "Chronic or acute?" "What body level is it on?"*
- **Emotions:** Worry and obsession; it is the seat of our ego so emotional problems are commonly the cause of indigestion. The pancreas connects with the sweetness, or lack of it, in our lives and may be considered a reflection of the balance between our giving and receiving and sweetness in life.
- **Chinese Medicine:** The stomach and pancreas, part of the earth element, are supported by earth and fire treatments, foods and supplements. The stomach, which receives and ripens ingested food and fluid, is called the "sea of food and fluid." The stomach is paired with the spleen and associated with the element=earth, season=summer, color=yellow, emo-tion= pensiveness, sound=singing, taste=sweet.

#5 Left— Liver

- **Location:** Right upper abdomen.
- **Function:** The liver, which Western medicine recognizes as having almost 1000 different functions, has two critical jobs of detoxifying our system and aiding in digestion.
- **Discussion:** The liver tests and identifies what has entered the system, neutralizing poisons, and creating needed blood, metabolic and immune constituents like bile, cholesterol, amino acids, etc.
- **Further Testing:** *"Is it a structural or functional problem?" "What body level is it on?"*
- **Emotions:** Anger, either excessive or inappropriate, or restrained and repressed. Dysfunction of the liver and gallbladder can also contribute to depression.
- **Chinese Medicine:** Chinese medicine considers the liver to be the organ that takes its orders from the gallbladder, moving blood, fluids, energy and emotions throughout the body. The liver rules flowing and spreading, stores the blood, rules the tendons and manifests in the nails; opens to the eyes. It is paired with the gallbladder and associated with the element=wood, season=spring, color=green or blue, emotion=anger, sound=shouting, flavor=sour.

#5 Right— Gallbladder

- **Location:** Sits behind the liver in the right hypochondriac area.
- **Function:** Aids in fat digestion.
- **Discussion:** Gallbladder dysfunction is one of the most common causes of digestive problems. Early symptoms include mild pain behind the right shoulder blade, abdominal bloating and gas. On a physical level, the gallbladder can affect almost any other part of the body and cause seemingly unrelated symptoms such as dizziness, headaches, sinusitis, tendon pain, leg pain, etc. As a result, the gallbladder and/or its meridian are often missed as the underlying cause of other

health problems. This organ empties into the common bile duct and if the duct becomes plugged, pain results due to the back up of fluids. The gallbladder is warm, damp and isolated with a poor blood supply so it can also become a good reservoir for chronic and sub-acute infection. If that happens each time a person eats, a little of the infecting agent is pumped into his or her system along with the bile, producing a slow, chronic poisoning action that strains the immune system.

- **Further Testing**: *"Functional or structural problem, or both?"* *"Type of blockage (stones, sludge, bacteria, etc)?"* *"Body level that the problem resides on?"*
- **Emotions**: The emotion of bitterness is associated with this organ. Dysfunction of the liver and gallbladder can also contribute to depression.
- **Chinese Medicine**: The gallbladder stores and secretes bile. It is said to rule decisions as the "commanding general of the body" and is paired with the liver which carries out those decisions. The gallbladder is associated with the element=wood, season=spring, color=green or blue, emotion= anger, sound=shouting, flavor=sour.

#6 Left— Kidney

- **Location**: At approximately waist level on both sides of the spine on the back.
- **Function**: These organs of excretion allow us to absorb helpful nutrients and excrete excess water and toxins.
- **Discussion**: Kidneys relate to our ability to flow with life as well as allowing life to flow through us. In Chinese medicine the kidneys have a close relationship with the lungs, and are considered to be the cause of deficiency-type asthma (where there is little phlegm production yet a lot of tightness and dry cough).
- **Further Testing**: *"Right, left or both?"* *"Function, structure or both?"* *"Body level affected?"*
- **Emotions**: Fear, indecisiveness, shame or repressed anger.

- **Chinese Medicine:** The kidneys store the *jing qi* (the *essence* provided by our parents at conception) and rule birth, development and maturation. They also rule water and bones, and open to the ears. Kidneys are paired with the urinary bladder and are associated with the element=water, season=winter, color=black or blue, taste=salty, emotion=fear, sound=groaning.

#6 Right— Urinary Bladder

- **Location:** Center of the lower abdomen.
- **Function:** The sack that holds urine until it is excreted.
- **Discussion:** The bladder is often a major component of back pain and tension because its acupuncture meridian runs from head to foot; at the neck the bladder meridian splits into a total of four energy lines which move run the back, then rejoin into two pathways at the buttocks, then move down the back of each leg to the sides of the feet to the little toes.
- **Further Testing:** *"Function or structure or both?" "Body level affected?"*
- **Emotions:** Control issues, or anxiety and holding onto old ideas.
- **Chinese Medicine:** The bladder receives and excretes the urine. It is paired with the kidneys and associated with the element=water, season=winter, color=black or blue, emotion=fear or being "pissed off," sound=groaning, taste=salty.

#7 Left— Other—Any other option not listed on the chart.

#7 Right— Endocrine

- **Locations:** Various parts of the body.
- **Function:** Regulates various functions in the body.
- **Discussion:** The endocrine system includes any of the hormone-producing organs. If this section tests positive, use your pendulum to determine *"Is it the entire system?"* or go

to the hormonal list in the *Descriptors* section to identify a specific gland. Note that the problem could also include chakra imbalances since they act like electric on/off switches for the hormonal glands.

- **Chinese Medicine:** The endocrine system is not specifically recognized in Traditional Chinese medicine (TCM) although a practitioner of TCM has methods that can be used to treat endocrine problems. For example:

  o **Adrenals** - as part of the water element, adrenals are supported by foods, herbs and supplements that support the other water elements - kidneys, bladder, lungs and large intestine.

  o **Thyroid and Thymus** - part of the fire element so these glands are supported by foods, herbs and therapies that support all fire element organs - heart, small intestine, triple warmer and heart constrictor. The fire element emotion is joy and is suppressed or controlled by the emotion of fear.

CHAPTER 19

PRSM Section A: Structural Factors

Introduction

The *Structural* section allows you to identify any structural area(s) of the body where a problem originates or is responding to an issue elsewhere. You can also refer to the box of identifiers to further define the exact tissue type - bone, muscle, lymph, scar, blood, etc. - that is affected by or causing the problem.

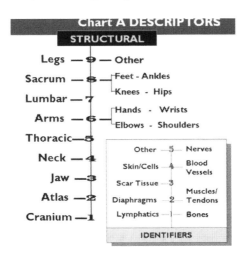

Figure 60 PRSM CHART *Section A Descriptors: Structural*

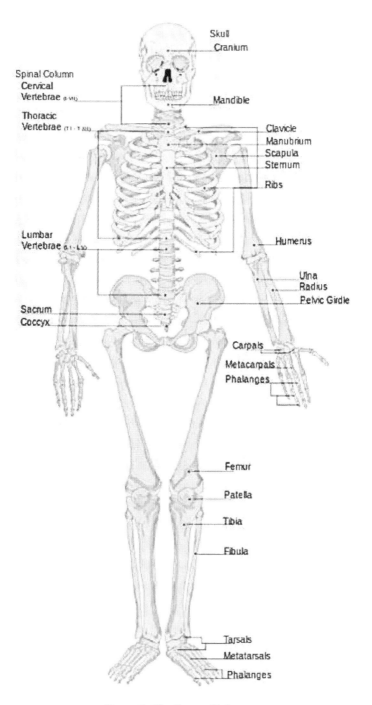

Figure 61 The Human Skeleton

Structural Descriptors

#1— Cranium

- **Location:** The skull bones that enclose the brain.
- **Discussion:** The major bones of the skull are the temporal, parietal, frontal, occipital, sphenoid, maxillary, mandible, and pterygoid. If cranium comes up in testing, it can mean all the bones are involved or it may only be one particular bone.
- **Further Testing:** *"Which particular bone or bone combination?" "Body level of the problem?" "Function, structure or both?"*
- **Emotions:** Feeling like being caught between a rock and a hard place.

#2— Atlas

- **Location:** The top vertebrae of the neck that allows the head to swivel. It is often referred to as C^0.
- **Discussion:** The brain stem passes through this vertebral opening so problems here can be especially devastating for the entire body.
- **Emotions:** Feeling the weight of the world on your shoulders; fear, confusion, running from life, not feeling supported.

#3— Jaw or Temporal-Mandibular Joint (TMJ)

- **Location:** Lower jaws and joints in front of the ears.
- **Discussion:** The jaw is a common problem in stressed or angry people who internalize their feelings. As a result they clench their teeth and may often need to use a night guard. Note that TMJ tightness can be a cause of sciatic nerve pain in the leg on the same side of the body because the sciatic nerve starts in the head near the jaw.
- **Further Testing:** *"Right, left or both sides?" "Body level?"*
- **Emotions:** Not speaking up, "bites back" his or her anger, resentment or desire for revenge.

#4— Neck

- **Location:** Cervical Spine Vertebrae (C1-7).
- **Discussion:** The second cervical is often a cause of laterality (left-right brain confusion). One sign of a C2 problem is that the protective energy field (the *wei chi*) is not centered on the body but skewed to either the left or the right.
- **Further Testing:** *"Which vertebra or combination is involved? "What body level?"*
- **Emotions:** Flexibility in attitudes and an ability to view things from other perspectives. Problems include a lack of communication, feeling overwhelmed or taking on too much responsibility.

#5— Thoracic

- **Location:** Vertebrae (T1-T12) running from the lowest neck vertebra to the lower back, just above the hips.
- **Discussion:** The T-1 vertebrae is most commonly associated with problems of head, neck and upper body due to a major nerve plexus (the thoracic inlet) located at this level. This nerve plexus sends branches to the heart, lungs, thyroid, arms, head and neck, chest and upper back. Each of the other vertebrae house nerves that connect to the various organs in the body. Because of this, problems in the vertebral column can also affect organ function or energy.
- **Further Testing:** *"Which vertebra or combination is involved?" "What body level?"*
- **Emotions:** Support in the form of love and people energy, responsibility, and the ability to support ideas.

#6 Left— Arms

- **Discussion:** This section tests positive for an entire arm as the problem (or causal) area.
- **Further Testing:** identify *"Left, right, or both?" "Body level?" "Upper?" "Lower?"*

- **Emotions:** Arms give us the ability to accept and give, so they represent being able to embrace life experiences.

#6 Right— Hands / Wrists / Elbows / Shoulders

- **Discussion:** This section tests positive if only part of the arm is involved.
- **Further Testing:** Identify *"Which part or parts are the problem area?"* by asking *"Is it the elbow?" "Hand?" "Wrist?" "Shoulder?" "Right or left?" "Both?" "Anything else?" "Body level?"*
- **Emotions:** The hands, wrists and arms give us an ability to grasp life experiences as well as allowing us to communicate, be creative and take responsibility for ourselves. Without hands or arms we cannot physically give or receive. Problems can also reflect being overwhelmed or as a way of avoiding responsibility. Joint problems represent changes in direction in life and the ease of those movements. Shoulder issues are about carrying life experiences joyously.

#7 Left— Lumbar

- **Location:** Lower back vertebrae (L1-5).
- **Discussion:** Nerves coming from this level are collected into the sciatic bundle and run down the legs.
- **Further Testing:** *"Which vertebrae?" "What body level?" "Bone problem?" "Nerve problem?"*
- **Emotions:** Support for our basic needs of food, shelter and clothing. Problems often result from repressed feelings and fears, repressed sexuality or financial worries.

#8 Left— Sacrum

- **Location:** Bottom section of the spine that forms a part of the pelvis.
- **Discussion:** The sacrum or tailbone is a collection of six bones that normally fuse into one as we grow. Occasionally the top bone is transitional, meaning it fails to fuse completely and is then considered the "6th lumbar." This transitional

bone leaves the lower back more prone to problems because of diminished stability.

- **Emotions:** Loss of power and old stubborn anger.

#8 Right— Feet / Ankles / Knees / Hips

- **Discussion:** This section will be positive if only part of an extremity is involved.
- **Further Testing:** Identify *"Which part or parts are the problem area?"* by asking, *"Feet?" "Ankles?" "Knees?" "Hips?" "Right, left or both?" "Anything else?" "What body level is involved?"*
- **Emotions:** Our ability to support ourselves, stability, grounding and balance, as well as our ability to move forward in life. Problems may reflect inflexibility, lack of self-support, uncertainty about one's life path, lack of strength, self-confidence or not feeling powerful.

#9 Left— Legs

- **Discussion:** This section tests positive if the entire leg is involved.
- **Further Testing:** *"Left, right, or both?" "Upper?" "Lower?"*
- **Emotions:** Legs represent our ability to move forward in life as well as to ground us.

#9 Right— Other

Any other structural element not listed on the *PRSM* CHART.

Structural Identifiers Descriptors

The *Structural Identifiers* help a practitioner to find the specific type of a structural problem and then to adjust his or her treatment approach in order to best address that particular problem. For example, if you are working with a client who tests for lumbar problems, it can help to know if the problem is with the muscles, nerves, or both.

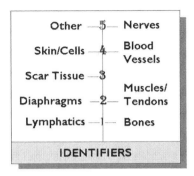

Figure 62 PRSM CHART: *Structural Identifiers*

#1 Left— Lymph System

- **Location**: Network of conduits throughout the body; considered a specialized component of the circulatory system.
- **Discussion**: In Western medicine, the lymphatic system of organs, ducts and nodes, helps to drain away waste matter and maintain the fluid balance of the internal body, as well as helping with immunity. In 2015, researchers discovered that the lymphatic system connects directly to the brain.
- **Emotions**: Being able to flow with life, to release the unnecessary (waste) and to bring nourishment to our cells. Problems should be a wake-up call to focus on the essentials of life.

#1 Right— Bones

- **Discussion**: Bones are the framework and foundation that support the entire body.
- **Emotions**: Strength, power and integrity; the structure of our life.
- **Chinese Medicine**: Bones are "ruled by the kidneys."

#2 Left— Diaphragms

- **Definition**: Diaphragms are body partitions of thin muscle and connective tissue.

- **Location:** There are two diaphragms in the pelvic cavity, one at the respiratory level of the solar plexus, one in the thoracic outlet across the top of the shoulders, and two in the head. We also have diaphragms in each joint (fingers, elbows, knees, etc.), and these are very prone to restrictions.
- **Function:** These thin muscles divide our bodies into functional cavities, while holding organs, blood vessels, nerves and lymph vessels in place.
- **Emotions:** Diaphragms are places of emotional holding causing health factors such as stiffness and pain as described by author Alexander Lowen in his book *Depression and the Body.*

#2 Right— Muscles/Tendons

- **Definition:** Muscles, contractile tissues of the body, are classified as skeletal, cardiac, or smooth (the latter found in the walls of organs). A tendon is fibrous connective tissue, linking muscle to the skeletal framework.
- **Location:** Throughout the body.
- **Function:** A muscle moves or checks the movement of a body part by contracting. A tendon unites a muscle with some other part and transmits the force exerted by the muscle.
- **Emotions:** Give us the ability to move and express our will-power and strength. Problems with the muscles and tendons indicate overbearing attitudes or a lack of will to move or change. They are our ability to move in life.

#3 Left— Scar Tissue

- **Definition:** Fibrous connective tissue that the body forms following an injury.
- **Location:** Wherever the body cells have been damaged by accidents, surgery, etc.
- **Function:** To repair injuries, cuts, surgeries or after dis-ease has taken place, then healed.
- **Discussion:** Scars can create actual physical blockages in a body and can obstruct energy flow through affected

acupuncture meridians or other areas. Also, sometimes tissue (a keloid scar) can continue growing inside the body, crowding out normal tissue and causing chronic pain.

- **Emotions**: Inability to let go.

#4 Left— Skin/Cells

- **Definition**: Skin is the two-layered covering of a vertebrate body consisting of an outer epidermis and an inner dermis.
- **Function**: Skin becomes a protective envelope covering our bodies. The cell forms the smallest structural unit of living matter capable of functioning independently.
- **Emotions**: Relationship to our own image and individuality. Problems connected to the skin include anger, fear or anxiety concerning a person's relationship to themselves and the world.
- **Chinese Medicine**: The skin is ruled by the lungs.

#4 Right— Blood Vessels

- **Location**: Throughout the body.
- **Function**: Transport blood to all parts of the body.
- **Emotions**: Represent achievement and wholeness.
- **Chinese Medicine**: Blood vessels are entitled the "*yang* organ of the *blood*" and carry both *qi* and *blood* throughout the body.

#5 Left— Other

- Something not found on this chart.

#5 Right— Nerves

- **Definition**: Nerves are filamentous bands of tissue that connect parts of the nervous system with the other organs, conducting nerve impulses. They are made up of axons and dendrites along with protective and supportive structures.
- **Location**: Throughout the body.
- **Emotions**: Acceptance.

CHAPTER 20

PRSM Section A: Emotional Factors

Introduction

Emotional Factors move us into less defined territory than other categories on the PRSM CHART. Here we take into account mental, emotional and physical scars, early childhood trauma, issues from past lives, and psychic attack. All these factors silently work on the physical body. Both our subconscious and superconscious minds register the past hurts all too well, and those energies carry into healthy tissue to create more dis-ease.

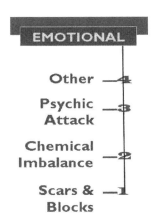

Figure 63 PRSM CHART *Section A Descriptors: Emotional*

Emotional Descriptors

#1— Scar or Blocks

- **Definition**: Patterns of emotional stress, created at a time when physical injury is coupled with emotional trauma, are called *engrams*.
- **Location**: Scar patterns are stored in injured tissue as cellular memory even after physical healing has taken place.
- **Discussion**: *Engrams* can reemerge later in a person's life as physical issues, reawakened by a combination of smell, sight, and or sound. For example, a child with a broken arm is taken to a hospital for care, where he experiences scary people (doctors and nurses dressed in white), strange hospital smells (such as rubbing alcohol), and experiences more pain (from shots and having the arm re-set before the cast went on). Many years later this now grown person might walk into a bar, see a man wearing a white sports jacket, smell the liquor, and suddenly find his arm hurting in the original break area. The cellular memory of the childhood trauma has reawakened due to this generalized combination of sensory input.

  Cellular memories can also be triggered when a person's soul recognizes another soul it had a traumatic experience with in a past life. The "victim" from that past encounter may feel uncomfortable or frightened for no apparent reason, or may experience an actual physical reaction such as pain or nausea.
- **Treatment**: These memory patterns can be cleared with a variety of methods such as LifeWeaving, acupuncture, Rolfing, Emotional Freedom Technique, deep-tissue massage, aromatherapy, or other methods that help release the stored emotions.

#2— Chemical Imbalance

- **Definition**: This is an actual physical imbalance in the body or brain chemicals that relay, amplify and modulate electrical signals passing between cells. These chemicals include serotonin, dopamine, norepinephrine, melatonin, insulin, and prostaglandins.

- **Discussion:** A chemical imbalance, which can lead to depression or insomnia, can be caused by problems in the brain or by the use of prescribed or recreational drugs affecting the chemical balance.

- **Treatment:** Depending on the source of the problem, the client may need to get off a drug or be placed on a supplement or a prescription drug for a while to help rebalance his or her brain chemicals.

#3— Psychic Attack

- **Definition:** Psychic attack refers to transference of negative energy from one person to another, to negative thought forms affecting a person, or to self-imposed negative elements.

- **Discussion:** Psychic attacks cannot happen unless the targeted person, due to fear, either consciously or unconsciously allows, or is open to, the process.

- **Treatment:** The best way to deal with psychic attack is to help the client strengthen his or her *wei qi* (the protective energy field) through visualization work, or to encourage them to carry or wear an object such as a cross or crystal, that he or she associates with increased protection. A person is also more prone to psychic attack when surrounded by clutter and disorder in his or her life so basic housecleaning and organization can be helpful.

#4— Other

- Any other emotional options not previously mentioned.

CHAPTER 21

PRSM Section A: Chakras

Introduction

The *Chakras*, an invisible energy system running up and down the spine, convert cosmic energy into an infinite, usable source of energy for the body.

Normally the chakras are about the size of a quarter but in times of stress or illness they can close down, open too far, or become partially clogged with debris-like thought forms or entities. If one or more of the chakras are shut down a person's energy is often low or illness can develop. Health problems caused by the chakra system usually affect the hormonal system first but will (depending on location), indirectly make an impact on other body organs as well. For example, headaches can be a result of the crown or brow chakras being either too open or too closed down.

On a subconscious level if a person shuts down in preparation for dying, both the root and crown chakras will often be closed.

Chakra Descriptors

Note that the chakra numbering system that is found both on the PRSM *Descriptors Section* and in this manual is not the traditional numbering system in use. I prefer to use the descriptive names/locations for the major chakras and have also included some important secondary chakras.

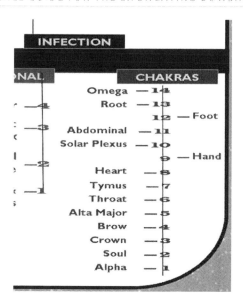

Figure 64 PRSM CHART *Section A Descriptors: Chakras*

#1— Alpha Chakra

- **Location:** Located eight inches above the spine.
- **Function:** Connects the lower bodies with their upper-dimensional counterparts. The Alpha chakra, working along with the Omega chakra, functions to allow for the enlightenment of the soul.
- **Color:** White

#2— Soul Chakra (Soul Star Chakra)

- **Location:** Above the head looking like a golden sun.
- **Function:** Extends light threads that connect us to our environment, our past, our present, and our destiny; gives us the will to evolve by giving an awareness of our soul and connecting the soul to the conscious self. It also gives perspective to the positive and negative events we experience on our soul's journey; holds all our memories from each lifetime, as well as all our flaws, which are then recreated into our next incarnation in order to heal them. The Soul chakra also controls all organs.

#3— Crown Chakra (7th Chakra; Third Ear)

- **Location:** Top of the head.
- **Function:** Purpose and spirituality. Regulates the inflow of information from the universe and represents acceptance and receiving.
- **Organs Affected:** Pineal gland, cerebral cortex, general nervous system and laterality (left-right brain synchronization).
- **Health Problems:** Headaches at the top or back of the head, stiff neck, a tendency not to listen, psychoses or brain dysfunction. A child who suffers from frequent colds and earaches - both symptoms that this chakra is blocked - should be allowed to share more in his or her own life in order to help heal.
- **Emotions:** Accepting yourself or receiving things from outside yourself; apathy, depression, bigoted, argumentative, closed emotionally, inability to learn.
- **Color:** Violet, pink or white.
- **Note/Tone:** B
- **Sound:** EEE
- **Element:** Cosmic energy
- **Chinese Medicine:** The location corresponds to the acupuncture point Governing Vessel 20 (GV20, *Baihui*).

#4— Brow Chakra (6th Chakra; Third Eye; Pineal)

- **Location:** Center of the forehead area between the eyebrows.
- **Function:** Intuition, imagination, vision and strategy. Gives us our visual clarity, vitalizes the lower part of the brain (the cerebellum and central nervous system), and enhances our creative and psychic abilities. This chakra represents our outer-directedness and sharing.
- **Organs affected:** Pineal and pituitary glands; carotid arteries, temples and forehead.

- **Health Problems:** Sinusitis, migraines, tension headaches, cataracts and other eye problems, lack of concentration, forgetfulness, tumors, strokes, seizures.
- **Emotions:** Not sharing fully and freely of yourself and your knowledge due to self-worth issues; being passive aggressive, preoccupied, nightmares, flighty.
- **Color:** Indigo or white light.
- **Note/Tone:** A
- **Sound:** AYE
- **Element:** Electrical or telepathic energy
- **Chinese Medicine:** The location corresponds to the extra acupuncture point (*Yintang*), midway between the eyebrows.

#5— Alta Major Chakra (Chandra; Mouth of the Goddess)

- **Location:** At the base of the skull, just above the point where the skull joins the neck.
- **Function:** It forms a center of communication between the Kundalini and the two head chakras. The alta major chakra is the anchor of the multi-dimensional energy structure of the individual, fused with the One and holding a crystal which allows the reception of information and spiritual energies. This chakra is very much connected with vision, both spiritually and physically. When balanced, it enhances intuitive ideas and somehow makes them more solid, tangible and achievable. This is also the working point for those who are telepathically gifted.
- **Organs Affected:** Linked to the pineal gland and the occipital area of the brain, which is, in turn, connected to the optic nerve.
- **Health Problems:** Dis-ease in this area may manifest as eye problems, floaters, cataracts, migraine, headaches and feelings of confusion, dizziness or a floating feeling, loss of sense of purpose, depression.
- **Color:** Bluish Violet
- **Element:** Air

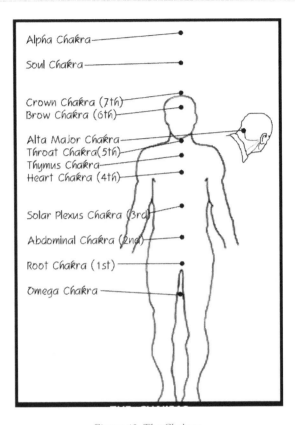

Figure 65 The Chakras

#6— Throat Chakra (5th Chakra)

- **Location:** At the throat.
- **Function:** Creativity, communication and guidance; allows us to have written and verbal expression, and prosperity. This chakra is the center of will, communication and relating.
- **Organs Affected:** Throat and mouth, cervical vertebrae, the parasympathetic nervous system, thyroid and parathyroid glands, vocal cords, neck and general skeletal activity.
- **Health Problems:** Dental, urges to smoke, throat cancer, hyper or hypothyroidism, colds, tonsillitis and sore throats, hearing problems, jaw problems, weak voice, laryngitis.
- **Emotions:** Inability to communicate, shy, tendency to control relationships, giving away too much control, emotional.

- Color: Blue or smoke grey.
- Note/Tone: G
- Sound: EYE
- Element: Ether
- Chinese Medicine: The location corresponds to the acupuncture point Conception Vessel #23 (CV23, *Lianquan*).

#7— Thymus Chakra (Etheric Heart or High Heart)

- Location: Between the heart and the throat on the upper chest.
- Function: Transpersonal chakra governing compassion, inner peace, and a connection to the world soul, divine love, forgiveness and the release of fear, voicing our true feelings. This chakra is considered the seat of the soul and relates to Christ Consciousness.
- Organs Affected: Thymus gland.
- Health Problems: Immune system in general.
- Emotions: Vulnerability and being too open; capability for social interaction. If the thymus Chakra is too open, it can lead to destructive or impure thoughts. If deficient, it leads to negative thoughts and an inability to move through one's limitations.
- Color: Turquoise, aquamarine or light teal blue.
- Note: F#
- Sound: HUL
- Element: Water
- Chinese Medicine: The location corresponds to the acupuncture point Conception Vessel #20 (CV20, *Huagai*).

#8— Heart Chakra (4th Chakra)

- Location: Center of the chest.
- Function: Relationships and healing. Represents a person's drive for love and self-esteem.
- Organs Affected: Heart, lungs, bronchi, trachea, breasts, immune and circulatory systems.
- Health Problems: Heart attack, strokes, asthma, lung or breast cancer, bronchitis, pneumonia, viral infections, rheumatoid

arthritis, upper back pain, blood dis-eases, compromised immune system.

- **Emotions:** An inability to express self-love; an inability to nurture yourself and others.
- **Color:** Green or deep red.
- **Note/Tone:** F
- **Sound:** AH
- **Element:** Air
- **Chinese Medicine:** The location corresponds to the acupuncture point Conception Vessel #17 (CV17, *Shanzong*).

#9— Hand Chakra

Figure 66 Hand Chakra

- **Location:** Close to the center of each hand.
- **Function:** Powerful sensors and channels for sending and receiving vibratory information and energy; the ability to channel internal love and artistic information to the external world.
- **Organs Affected:** Hands and arms. Hand chakras are also connected to the heart chakra.
- **Health Problems:** Chronic cold hands; artistic blocks. If constantly open, these chakras can affect joints and muscles of the hands making them weaker than usual and clumsy (often the heart chakra is too open as well). Hand chakras that are too closed down, can lead to stiff and swollen joints.

- **Emotions:** Difficulties taking hold or relating to one's life; being unable to give and receive; trust and control issues.
- **Color:** Gold (left hand - receiving) and white or silver (right hand - giving).
- **Sound:** None recognized.
- **Element:** Ether
- **Chinese Medicine:** Corresponds to the acupuncture point Heart #8 (H8, *Shaofu*).

#10— Solar Plexus Chakra (3rd Chakra; Power)

- **Location:** Over the upper abdomen in the navel area.
- **Function:** Represents the seat of self-identity (ego), self-expression, personal power, mentality and structure.
- **Organs Affected:** Stomach and pancreas, liver and kidneys, adrenals, gallbladder, muscles and nervous system, skin, diaphragms (and breath).
- **Health Problems:** Stomach ulcers, stomach cancer, diabetes, liver and kidney dis-ease, adrenal exhaustion, digestive and back problems.
- **Emotions:** Power and will, self-esteem and self-confidence, self-respect. Unrealistic or overinflated view of the self, narcissism or self-hate, domination, anger and abuse of others (excess); or being cowardly, meek and submissive, loss of personal power; conflicts between ego and one's own identity; one's inability to express one's self (deficiency).
- **Color:** Yellow or black.
- **Note/Tone:** E
- **Sound:** OH
- **Element:** Fire
- **Chinese Medicine:** Corresponds to the acupuncture point Conception Vessel #12 (CV12, *Zhongwen*).

#11— Abdominal Chakra (2nd Chakra; Sexual; Spleen)

- **Location:** In the lower abdomen three inches below the navel.

- **Function:** Represents wants, desires, feelings and creativity.
- **Organs Affected:** Bowels, appendix, uterus, lower back, gonads, mammary glands, sexuality and sensual emotions.
- **Health Problems:** Menstrual, bowel, irritable bowel syndrome, appendicitis, yeast infection, lumbar pain, diarrhea or constipation, spleen or bladder issues.
- **Emotions:** Wanting everything (excess); denying one's own wants and letting everyone else's needs come first (deficiency); addiction, frigidity, jealousy or possessiveness.
- **Color:** Orange.
- **Note/Tone:** D
- **Sound:** OOO
- **Element:** Water
- **Chinese Medicine:** Corresponds to the acupuncture point Conception Vessel #5 (CV5, *Shimen*).

#12— Root Chakra (1st Chakra)

- **Location:** At the base of the spine.
- **Function:** Represents wants and survival; grounding and creative power; vitality, strength, money, security, karma.
- **Organs Affected:** Coccyx, sexual organs, urinary bladder, nervous system, organs of elimination, skeletal system, teeth, and lower extremities.
- **Health Problems:** Anything dealing with the above organs including arthritis, constipation, knee problems, hemorrhoids, or weight issues.
- **Emotions:** Inadequate expression or acceptance of needs, clinging; an inability to release the past; possessiveness; anger, fear, fight/flight response.
- **Color:** Red.
- **Note/Tone:** C
- **Sound:** UH
- **Element:** Earth

- Chinese Medicine: Corresponds to the acupuncture point Governing Vessel #1 (GV1, *Huiyin*).

#13— Foot Chakra

Figure 67 Foot Chakra

- Location: Close to the center of the sole of each foot.
- Function: Grounds us to the Earth, thus allowing us to receive Earth energy and to act on this planet in real time as a grounded spirit. The foot chakra also allows us to drain stress, fatigue and body disharmony into the Earth.
- Organs Affected: Feet and legs; entire body.
- Health Problems: Chronically cold feet, muscle spasms in legs. If too open, a person may be clumsy or often strain ankles and knees. If too closed down, there is a tendency for injuries of the foot, leg, or lower body; tight and inflexible legs and feet; wide temperature swings in the feet.
- Emotions: Unable to ground oneself to reality.
- Color: Burgundy
- Sound: None recognized
- Element: Earth
- Chinese Medicine: Corresponds to the acupuncture point Kidney #1 (K1, *Taiyin*).

#14— Omega Chakra

- Location: Eight inches below the spine.

- Function: The Omega chakra, along with the Alpha, acts as a body anchor - the Alpha connects the lower bodies with their upper-dimensional counterparts. Also the Omega anchors the lower bodies across a special grid of incarnations. The Alpha and Omega chakras function together to allow enlightenment of the soul.
- Omega Color: Black
- Element: Cosmic Energy

Working with the Chakras

The chakras can be treated by many methods including visualization, colors, acupuncture, pendulum releases, sound therapy or essential oils to name a few, as well as the technique presented below:

Counter-Balancing Technique

- If a chakra is closed down - apply more of the same energy in the form of colors, sound or food.
- If a chakra is open too wide - remove identical colors, or counteract by applying the opposite chakra color. To use this counterbalancing technique, note that:
  - The crown chakra counteracts the root
  - The brow chakra counteracts the abdominal
  - The throat chakra counteracts the solar plexus
  - The heart and thymus stand alone

To use the counterbalancing method to sedate or quiet down a chakra, apply the color of the opposite chakra to the one that is too strong. For example, if the brow chakra (violet) is too open, apply the abdominal chakra color orange in the form of orange-colored foods or clothing, or use the abdominal chakra sound, etc. to counterbalance.

CHAPTER 22

PRSM Section B: Deaths - How and Why

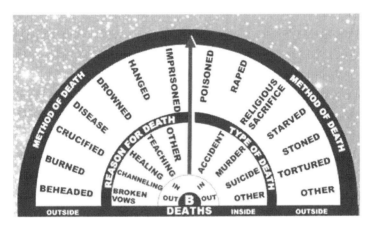

Figure 68 PRSM CHART *Section B: Deaths*

Introduction

The *Deaths* chart can be used to determine the reason for, method of, and type of past deaths or injuries. This information is not always necessary if you are doing LifeWeaving clearing but it can be helpful for understanding symptoms that a client is currently experiencing such as weight issues (starved), neck pain (beheaded or hanged), fear of water (drowned), unable to wear a turtle neck sweater (hanged), allergic to grass (died in a grass fire), etc.

Elements of *Chart B*

1—Category of death or injury occurred

- Accident
- Murder
- Suicide
- Other

2—Why Killed or Injured

- Broken Vows
- Channeling
- Teaching
- Other

3—Method of Death or Injury

- Beheaded
- Burned
- Crucified
- Disease
- Drowned
- Hanged
- Imprisoned
- Poisoned
- Raped
- Religious Sacrifice
- Starved
- Stoned
- Tortured
- Other

Note that since the end of 2014, I use this section more for general clearing of any past life death cell memories rather than for researching specific deaths.

PRSM *Section B* Protocols

To learn more about a past life death:

1. Place the client's *Personal Trinity* and your pendulum on the neutral line of this section.
2. Ask *"How did the person die?"*
3. Ask *"Why were they killed?"*
4. Ask *"What was the method of death or injury?"*

To simply clear all cell memory of past life deaths:

1. Place the client's *Personal Trinity* and your pendulum on the neutral line of this section.
2. Allow your pendulum to circle over *Section B* and ask that all cell memories of past deaths be brought to the lower conscious mind and sent directly into the basket until the *Clearing Macro* is run.

Remember that this section of the PRSM CHART is not needed for diagnostic purposes, but can be helpful for explaining a client's presenting complaint or fears.

Critical Differences Between Standard and LifeWeaving Dowsing

Several aspects of LifeWeaving dowsing are different than the general pendulum and chart techniques found in the literature. Below are some extremely important dowsing tips that will help ensure your work with these charts will be accurate.

Harmonize the *Personal Trinity*—The Self, Soul and Ego

Rather than filtering answers through a person's High Self as is the practice in regular dowsing, in LifeWeaving the invocation is used to first harmonize the client's *Personal Trinity*: his/her Ego, Self and Soul (High Self Committee), and then to align this trinity with the Divine Plan. By working with all parts of the *Personal Trinity* we can receive input from our most wounded part - the Ego and our strong-willed Self that is in charge of decision-making. Here are the parts of the *Personal Trinity*:

o **The Ego** strongly influences the physical body (especially the three lower chakras) by responding primarily to fears and memories in matters of safety for the physical body, often getting attention through physical signals such as pain or emotions.

o **The Human Self**, which operates out of the heart chakra, sits between Ego and Soul and receives information to be considered and potentially acted upon. It has a large influence on health due to its use of free will and decision making.

○ **The Soul/High Self** is concerned with spiritual development and relates more to the three upper chakras.

Before beginning a dowsing session bring the *Personal Trinity* into *"perfect harmony, cooperation and agreement"* by reciting the *Invocation* found on the POWER CHART.

Alternately, a practitioner can use the following protocol to harmonize the *Personal Trinity*:

1. Test the percentage that the Self and Soul are in harmony. If not at 100%, use the LifeWeaving process to find and clear all reasons to bring them into 100% alignment.

2. Test what percentage the Ego is in harmony with this (now) aligned Self/Soul. Continue to research and clear until it reaches 100%.

3. Ask to connect this harmonized *Personal Trinity* to the Divine Plan and make sure it is at 100%.

▪ **Each Dowsing Sequence Begins on a Neutral Line.** Always start your testing by placing your pendulum into a gentle neutral swing over the red neutral line on a *Chart Key* or *Chart Section*, then, with intention, add in the client and the issue to be cleared.

▪ **Each Dowsing Sequence Ends on the Neutral Line** 'Train' your pendulum to return to the neutral line of the section you are testing after it finds all necessary *Keywords*. This confirms that your pendulum is finished with that section.

▪ **Allow for Multiple Answers.** Always allow for your pendulum to find more than one word at a time (if there are any) as you test a section.

▪ **When Dowsing a Section is Completed, Return to the Chart Key.** When your pendulum returns to and remains on neutral for a specific section, go back to the *Chart Key* neutral line to find your next action: to dowse another section on that chart, to switch to another chart, or to take your findings to the *Clearing Macro*. (Note that occasionally you may be directed to go back to the same section right away.)

- **Create an Imaginary Basket to Hold Answers Until Ready to Clear**. As you find the *Keywords* necessary to clear a blockage, have the client place them in an imaginary basket above his/her head until all are found for that particular topic. Let them know that once the *Keywords* have been added to the basket, spirit remembers them so the client does not have to. When your pendulum indicates *Clearing Macro* on the *Chart Key*, have the client envision *"spiraling them together and down through the mind, body and spirit..."*. The complete *Clearing Macro* is found on the RESEARCH CHART.

- **Recognize that a New Layer is Ready to Clear**. As you say the *Clearing Macro*, allow your pendulum to move in a gentle neutral swing over the neutral line. If the pendulum drops off the line to the left of neutral, it indicates that another layer is ready to come up for research and clearing. If this happens, place the same issue you have been working on onto the neutral line and repeat the LifeWeaving process for the client.

  Note: A drop to the right of neutral means that the client's assigned spirit helpers have the problem and need to be cleared). Say: *"Educate, elevate, remove or replace,"* then retest that the problem has cleared.

- **Test Variations on the Original Issue**. Once a statement or issue is at neutral, you should also try testing different but similar aspects of the problem. For example, after testing the word 'diabetes', you can try 'high blood sugar', 'glucose', 'insulin resistance', 'sugar problems,' etc.

- **Do a Final Completion Check After Clearing**. As part of the *Completion Check*, test each part of the *Personal Trinity* (i.e., Ego, Self,

Soul) separately as occasionally one may only be a little out of balance and its signal is overwhelmed by the other (stronger) parts. Finally test the client's assigned spirit guides and guardian angels and other spirits as well for neutrality/completion.

APPENDIX TWO

The Worksheet

MASTER LIFEWEAVING WORKSHEET

☐ REPORT SENT ☐ AMT. BILLED ☐ PAID | DATE REQUEST REC'D

PHYSICAL COMPLAINTS / ISSUES OF CONCERN / PHRASES TO CLEAR:

NAME:

PHONE #:

E-MAIL:

TREATMENT DATE:

WORK START TIME: FINISHED: MINUTES:

PHONE START FINISHED: MINUTES:

CHECK LIST FOR PREPAREDNESS (INVOCATION SHOULD HAVE CLEARED ALL TO "YES")

1. Ego, Self and Soul are 100% in harmony. YES NO
2. Personal Trinity and Divine Plan are 100% aligned. YES NO
3. One Spirit comprises the Self. YES NO
4. Soul Committee size is 9-99 (prefer 9 or 11). YES NO
5. Spirit helpers are God-sanctioned. YES NO
6. Spirit helpers are all on committees. YES NO
7. All spirit helpers vibrate at infinity. YES NO
8. All body levels are aligned, cleared, and balanced. YES NO
9. All chakras are aligned, cleared, and balanced. YES NO
10. No cords or attachments. YES NO
11. No entities or openings that shouldn't be there. YES NO

SUPPLEMENTAL TESTING (USE AS NEEDED):

1. ☐ Fast-track soul? ☐ Slow-track soul?
2. Number of concurrent Lives? ____
3. % Incarnated? ____% At an exit point? YES NO
4. 'Spirit work elsewhere' at 20% or less? YES NO
5. All Life Areas aligned, cleared, & balanced? YES NO
6. Energy Makeup: Angelic Energy ____% Human Energy ____% Elemental Energy ____% Type: Earth Air Water Fire Ether
7. Soul Consciousness Level now? ____ /12.12. Energy? ____
8. % Aligned with Original Perfect Destiny Blueprint? ____
9. % Aligned with Original Perfect Health Blueprint? ____
10. Spirit helpers have something to bring up? YES NO

STATEMENT BEING CLEARED	CONTROL TO CK INSTEAD PERCEPTION	KEY WORDS to take to THE CLEARING MACRO	EGO	SELF	SOUL	ASSIGND OTHERS	BODY LEVEL

FINAL CHECK

Figure 69 LifeWeaving Worksheet, Front

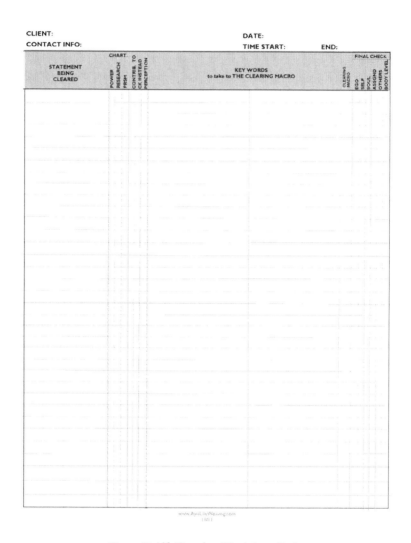

Figure 70 LifeWeaving Worksheet, Back

The worksheet is available for free download at
www.AyniLifeWeaving.com

Bibliography

Aivanhov, Omraam Mikhael
*A New Earth---Methods, Exercises, Formulas and Prayers 4th Edition,
Complete Works - Volume 13* (France: Editions Prosveta, 1992)

Archangel Ariel and Tashira Tachi-ren
What Is Lightbody? (Little Springs, Georgia: World Tree Press, 1999)

Blackburn, Gabriele
Science and the Art of Pendulum---A Complete Course in Radiesthesia
(Ojai, CA: Idywild Books, 1983)

Bletzer, June G., Ph.D.
The Donning International Encyclopedic Psychic Dictionary (West
Chester, Pennsylvania: Whitford Press, 1986)

Brennan, Barbara A.
Hands of Light: A Guide to Healing Through The Human Energy Field
(NYC, NY: Bantam Books, 1987)

Capra, Fritjof
The Tao of Physics (Berkely: Shambala Press, 1975)

Cohen, Neil S.
*Attitudinal Awareness Guide---Emotional / Attitudinal Causes of
Physical Problems* (Mount Shasta, CA: Legion of Light Products, 1989)

Conlon, Carole
A Manual for Fifth Dimensional Healing---LifeWeaving the Spirit
(Albuquerque, NM: AyniWrite Press 2008)

Conlon, Carole
PRSM Pendulum Research Sourcing Method---LifeWeaving the Body
(Albuquerque, NM: AyniWrite Press 2009)

de Flores, Bryan
Masterworks (Las Vegas, Nevada: LightQuest International, 2006)

Detzler, Robert
Soul Re-Creation---Developing Your Cosmic Potential (Redmond, WA: SRC Publishing, 1994)

Detzler, Robert
Your Mind-Net---Reprogramming the Subconscious (Redmond, WA: SRC Publishing, 1988)

Friedman, Norman
Bridging Science and Spirit---Common Elements in David Bohm's Physics, The Perennial Philosophy and Seth (St. Louis, MO: Living Lake Books, 1990)

Funk & Wagnalls
Standard Dictionary of the English Language International Edition, VOL. I & II (New York: Funk & Wagnalls Publishing Co., Inc., 1973)

Grabhorn, Lynn
Dear God! What's Been Happening to Us? (Charlottesville, VA: Hampton Roads Publishing Co., Inc., 2003)

Hall, Manly P.
Healing---The Divine Art (Los Angeles, CA: Philosophical Research Society, 1995)

Hawkins, David R., M.D.
Power vs. Force, An Anatomy of Consciousness---The Hidden Determinants of Human Behavior (Sedona, AZ: Veritas Publishing, 1995)

Hawkins, David R., M.D.
The Eye of the I---From Which Nothing is Hidden (Sedona, AZ, Veritas Publishing, 2001)

Hawkins, David R, M.D.
I---Reality and Subjectivity (Sedona, AZ: Veritas Publishing, 2003)

Leadbeater, C.W.
Man Visible Invisible---Examples of Different Types of Men As Seen by Means of Trained Clairvoyance (Wheaton, IL: The Theosophical Publishing House, 1925)

Leadbeater, C.W.

The Inner Life (Wheaton, IL: Theosophical Publishing House, 1978)

Leadbeater, C.W. & Besant, A.

Thought-Forms (Wheaton, Il: Theosophical Publishing House, 1971)

Longren, Sig

The Pendulum Kit (NYC, NY: Simon & Schuster, Inc., 1990)

Luppi, Diana and Mission Control

E.T. 101--- The Cosmic Instruction Manual (Santa Fe, NM: Intergalactic Council Publications, 1990)

Kinnear, Willis (ed)

Spiritual Healing---The Art and Science of Meditation (Los Angeles, CA: Science of Mind Publications, 1983)

McLaren, Karla

Your Aura and Your Chakras---The Owner's Manual (New Dehli India: Motilal Banarsidass Publ., 2000)

Monte, Tom and the Editors of East-West Natural Health

World Medicine---The East West Guide to Healing Your Body (NYC, NY: Putnam Publishing Group, 1993)

Myss, Caroline

Sacred Contracts---Awakening Your Divine Potential (New York: Harmony Books, 2001)

Neil, Penny R.N., M.S. (Ed.)

Contact Reflex Analysis and Applied Trophology---A Healing Art Researched, Developed and Taught by Dr. D.A. Versendaal (1976)

Nielson, Greg

Beyond Pendulum Power---Entering the Energy World (Reno, NV: Conscious Books, 1988)

Nielson, Greg and Polansky, Joseph

Pendulum Power (Rochester, VT: Destiny Books, 1977)

Newton, Michael, Ph.D.
Journey of Souls---Case Studies of Life Between Lives (St. Paul, Minnesota: Llewellyn Publications, 1996)

Olson, Dale
Advanced Pendulum Instruction and Applications Vol. 1 (Eugene, OR: Crystalline Publications, 1991)

Starr, Jelaila
We are the Nibiruans---Return of the 12th Planet Book One (The Nibiruan Council, 2003)

Talbot, Michael
Holographic Universe (New York: Harper Perennial, Division of Harper Collins Publishers, 1991)

Wallace, Amy and Henkin, Bill
The Psychic Healing Book (Oakland, CA: Wingbow Press, 1978)

Villoldo, Ph.D., Alberto,
Mending the Past and Healing the Future with Soul Retrieval (California: Hay House, Inc., 2005)

Index

12th dimension, 112
17th dimension, 109
1st chakra. *See* root chakra
2nd chakra. *See* abdominal chakra
3rd chakra. *See* solar plexus chakra
3rd dimension, 112
4th chakra. *See* Heart Chakra
5th chakra. *See* Throat Chakra
5th element. *See* elements, ether
6th chakra. *See* Brow Chakra
6th lumbar, 182
7th chakra. *See* Crown Chakra
abdomen, 153, 168, 169,170, 171,
    174, 198, 200
    bloating, 172
    pain, 161
abdominal chakra, 23, 198, 201
accountant archetype. *See* scribe
    archetype
aches and pains, unexplained, 149
activities section, 15, **24**, 25
actor archetype. *See* artist arche-
    type
acupuncture meridians, 37, 136,
    185
addict archetype, 45
adrenaline, 152
adrenals, 37, 135, **152**, 156, 175,
    exhaustion, 198
advocate archetype, 45
affairs of the bedroom, 152
affected areas of life, 93
affected areas of the body or
    mind, 93
affirmations, 15, **25**, 26
AIDS, ix, 37, 135, 157, **161**
AIDS-related complex (ARC), 37,
    135, **161**

Akashic records, 106
alchemist archetype, 46
allergy, 37, 135, **144**, 203
    descriptors, 144
    quick testing for, 145, 146
alpha chakra, 23, 136, **192**, 200
alta major chakra, 23, 136, **194**
alternate time, 99
amalgam fillings, 144, 166
Amazon archetype. See warrior
    archetype
ambassador archetype. See
    mediator archetype
ancestral time, 99
anemia, 168
angel archetype, 41, **46**
angelic kingdom, 22, 31, **32**
angels, 32, 33, 96, 99
anger, 93, 169, 182, 185, 198, 199
    and infection, 157, 159, 160
    and liver/gallbladder, 153,
        172, 173
    not spoken, 166, 179
    towards a partner, 152
    towards God, 156
anti-inflammatory, 153
anxiety, 153, 154,169, 174, 185
appendicitis, 199
appendix, 37, 136, 169, 199
apprentice archetype. See student
    archetype
arbitrator archetype. See judge
    archetype
ARC. *See* Aids-Related Comples
archangels, 13, 21, **22**, 32
    Archangel Chamuel, 32
    Archangel Michael, 32, 101,
        106, 112

Archangel Uriel, 32
Archeangel Raphael, 32
archetypes, 39, 40
    and healing and clearing
        work, 42, 43
    blocks, 104
    definitions and energy pic-
        tures, 44 - 83
    shadow, **40, 41**, 44
    testing protocol, 43
    using the chart, 43
architect archetype. *See* engineer
    archetype
Aristotle, 20
arms, 180, 181,188,197
arthritis, 197, 199
arthropods, 158, 159
artist archetype, 47
artistic blocks, 197
ascended masters, 13, **22**
ascension, xvi, 35, 104
    block, 104
assigned spirit helpers. *See* spirit
    helpers
asthma, 173, 196
astral body, **34, 137**, 157
athlete archetype, 47
atlas, 179
Atman body, **34**, 35, 137, 138
attorney archetype. *See* advocate
    archetype
autonomic nervous system, 155
avatar, **22**, 102
avenger archetype, 48
avenging angel archetype. *See*
    avenger archetype
back problems, 198
bacteria, 37, 135, 157, 158, **159**,
    160, 173
Baihui, 193
bardo, 98

basket, holding, 4, 6, 9, 18, 88, 92,
    104, 110, 112, 205, 209
Becker-Hagens Grid Map, 148
beggar archetype, 48
beliefs, 13, 28, 51, 100, 118, **119**
    and dis-ease, 117, 118
    core, 105
    in LifeWeaving System, 94
benefit, 106
    block, 104
    programs, 93, 94,104
benign tumor, 161, 162
Besant, 107
bigoted, 193
bile, 156, 172, 173
    duct, 160, 168, 172
Black Lines, 148
black widow archetype. *See*
    femme fatale archetype
bladder, urinary, 136, **174**, 175,
    199
    meridian, 174
    problems, 199
Blessing Seal, 109, 110
bloating, 159, 161, 172
blocks, 88, 94, 103, 118, 131, 185,
    188, 193, 209
    and the clearing macro, 112
    Chart B section, 104 - 108
    emotional, xv, xvi, 3, 4, 26,
        34, 38, 101, 102, 120,
        121, 132, 136
    energetic, 36, 101, 104, 168
blood, 104, 105, 151, 160, 161,
    168, 169, 170, 172, 173, 177,
    185
    disease, 168, 197
    pressure, 156, 168
    sugar, regulation, 156, 209
    vessels, 38, 136, 168, 184,
        185

body categories, PRSM, 29, 37
body elemental, 22
body levels, 29, 33, 34, 88, 120,
  125, 128, 157, 159-162, 168,
  169, 171-174, 179-182
  and perception, 108
  and the clearing macro, 112,
    113
  in the dis-ease process, 119,
    120, 136, 137
  mental, 35, 117, 120, 125,
    138
  physical, 12, 22, 30, 34, 100,
    107, 117, 138
  PRSM Chart section, 125,
    128, 130
  spiritual, 35, 100, 121
bone, 19, 38, 136, 140, 152, 167,
  174, 177, 179, 181, 182, **183**
  health, 153
  marrow, 152
bowels, 154, 199
brain, 37, 135, 138, 156, **166**, 179,
  183, 194
  and T-1, 154
  chemicals, 188, 189
  dysfunction, 180, 193
  stem, 155, 156, 179
breasts, 152, 196
bromine, 146
bronchi, 37, 136, 196
  and lungs, 169
  bronchitis, 196
brow chakra, 23, 191, **193**, 201
Buddha, 22
Buddhic body, 137, 138
builder archetype. *See* engineer
  archetype
builders of form, 32
bully archetype, 49
calcium uptake or loss, 153

call upon/use, 15, **21**
Campbell, Joseph, 40
cancer, 37, 120, 135, 149, 157,
  161, 162
  breast, 196
  lung, 196
  stomach, 198
  throat, 195
candidiasis, 160
carbohydrate, 144, 155
caregiver archetype. *See* healer
  archetype
cataracts, 194
celebate archetype. *See* monk/nun
  archetype
cell, 19, 38, 118, 136, 153-155,
  161, 170, 183, 184, **185**, 189
  memories, 95, 104, 188, 204,
    205
  memory blocks, 104
  metabolism regulation, 154
cellular
  level of consciousness, 36
cerebellum, 193
cerebral cortex, 193
cerebrospinal system, 137
cervical spine, 180, 195
  adjustments not holding,
    155
  and laterality, 180
chakras, 15, **23**, 34, 38, 136, 137,
  191
  abdominal, 23, **198**, 201
  alpha, 23, 136, **192**, 200
  alta major, 23, 136, **194**
  and endocrine system, 151,
    174
  and the spine, 23
  counterbalancing, 18, **201**
  crown, 23, 191, **193**, 201
  brow, 23, 191, **193**, 201

descriptors, 191

foot, 136, **200**

heart, 13, 23, 196, **197**, 201

hand, 23, 136, **197**

imbalance, 174

omega, 23, 136, 192, **200**

root, 24, **199**, 201

solar plexus, 23, **198**, 201

soul, 23, 136, **192**

three lower and the ego, 12, 207

three upper and high self, 13, 208

throat, 23, **195**, 201

thymus, 23, **196**, 201

chandra chakra. *See* alta major chakra

Chang, Stephen, 151

Chart Key, xv, 6, **9**, 15, 26, 33, 43, 44, 88, 92, 110, 125, 161, 208, 209

check for preparedness, 6, 14

check instead, 89, 92, **99**, 100

check the environment, 100

cheese allergy, 145

chef archetype. *See* hedonist archetype

chemicals, 12, 34, 38, 135, 136, 143, **146**, 147, 158, 166

hormone-disrupting, 146

imbalance, 38, 136, **188, 189**

Research Chart A, descriptors, 146

chest, 167, 169, 180, 196

child archetypes, 49, 50, 51, 52

chlorine, 146

choose a positive outcome, 94

Christ consciousness, 196

circulatory system, 153, 183, 196

clearing activity, 24

clearing macro, vii, 4, 6, 7, 21, 88, 92, 105, 106, 107, **111**, 112, 205, 209

protocol, 113

clown archetype, 41, **53**

clumsy, 197, 200

coccyx, 199

codependency, 82

cold hands, chronic, 197

colds, 195

earaches in child, 193

colitis, 154

collective, 40, 97

color, 9, 15, **18**, 23, 32, 102, 168, 169, 171-175, 192-194, 196-201

correction method, 18, **19**, 201

commanding general of the body, 173

companion archetype, 53

Completion Check, 6, 7, 88, 111, **113**, 209

protocol, 113

con artist archetype. *See* thief archetype

concussion, 166

confusion, 194, 179, 180

conscious mind, 17, 30, 34, 41-43, 105, 118, 119, 134, 137, 159

lower, 205

constipation, 159, 199

contracts/vows, **94**, 97, 101, 104, **105**, 107, 204

contributing factors, 6, 89, 100, 126, 131, 132

contributing to, 89

control issues, 174

cords, 104, **105**

core beliefs, 105

cosmic element, 193, 201

Cota-Robles, Patricia, 138
coughing when older, 155
counselor archetype. *See* mentor
   archetype, *See* healer archetype, *See* advocate archetype
coward archetype. *See* bully
craftsperson archetype. *See* artist
   archetype
cranium, 179. *See also* skull
creativity/children life area, 17
critic archetype. *See* judge archetype
critical parent archetype, 41, 42,
   54
Crohn's Disease, 154
crown chakra, 23, 191, **193**, 201
cultural level of consciousness, 36
Curry Lines, 148
curses, 104, **106**
"*curses, contracts, heart vows, hidden
vows, soul programs*", 101, 107
CV5, 199
CV12, 198
CV17, 197
CV20, 196
CV23, 196
damsel archetype, 42, **54**, 73
dark entities, 12, 97, 100
dark forces, 12
defender archetype. *See* advocate
   archetype
dental problems, 166, 195
Depression and the Body, 184
descriptors. *See* PRSM, descriptors
designer archetype. *See* Engineer
   archetype
destroyer archetype, 55
detective archetype, 55
Detzler, Robert, xiii
devas, 32

diabetes, 198, 209
diagnosis, 116, 118, 119
   PRSM protocol, **125**, 132
diaphragms, 38, 136, **184**, 198
diarrhea, 159, 161, 171, 199
digestion, 171, 172, 198
dimensions, iii, 31, 33, 109, 112,
   113, 192, 200
   multi, 3, 194
   inter, 23
dioxin, 146
diplomat archetype. *See* mediator
   archetype
directional ring, **15**, 16, 29, 92
discarnate, 96, **106**, 121
disciple archetype. *See* student
   archetype
disclaimer, 116
diverticulitis, 154
Divine Body, 139
Divine Plan, iii, 5, 14, 134, 135,
   207, 208
divine self. *See I AM* presence
dizziness, 172, 194
DNA, 19, 33, 99
Do Mental Work, 100
Do Physical Work, 100
Don Juan archetype, 56
door of the lungs, 167
dowsing questions, 92
dreamer archetype, 42, 56
dry cough, 173
duality, 35, 97, 139
ear, 166, 167, 174, 179
   third, 23, 193
earth element, 20, 21, **32**, 34, 136,
   171, 199, 200
edema, 154
"*educate, elevate, remove and
replace*", 13, 14, 101, 145, 209

EENT, 37, 135, **166**

ego, **12**, 13, **30**, 40, 41, 95, 96, 134, 198, 207

    seat of, 172

ego, self, soul. *See Personal Trinity*

electrical, 37, 135

electromagnetic, 136, 148

    descriptors, 146

elements, 15, 19, 23

    air element, **20**, 21, 32, 34, 137, 194, 197

    cosmic, 193, 201

    earth, **20**, 21, 34, 136, 171, 199, 200

    ether, **20**, 196, 198

    fire, **21**, 35, 138, 168, 175, 198

    metal, 169

    telepathic/electrical, 194

    water, **20**, 35, 137, 174, 175, 196, 199

    wood, 172, 173

elemental kingdom, 31, 32

elementals, xiv, 21, 22, 31, 106

    personal body, **22**, 32

    types, 32

emotional body category, 29, **37**, 38, 125

emotional body level, 35, 120, **137**

emotions, 20, 42

    ability for nurturing; compassion, 168

    ability for social interaction, 196

    ability to communicate, 181

    ability to flow with life, 173, 182, 183

    ability to get rid of waste in your life, 169

    ability to give and receive, 152, 181, 193

    ability to grasp life experiences, 181

    ability to move and express willpower and strength, 184

    ability to move forward in life, 182

    ability to release unnecessary, 183

    ability to support ourselves, 182

    ability to support ideas, 180

    acceptance, 186

    achievement and wholeness, 185

    addiction, 199

    anger, 153

        excessive/inappropriate, 172

        not spoken, 166, 179

        restrained or repressed, 172

        tiny bits of, 157

    anxiety about relating to the world, 185

    apathy, 193

    argumentative, 193

    avoiding responsibilty, 181

    being overwhelmed, 181

    bigoted, 193

    bitterness; hard thoughts; condemning, 161, 173

    carrying life experiences joyously, 181

    changes in direction in life and the ease of those movements, 181

    clinging, 199

    connection to the outside world, 166

    controlling in relationships, 195

    cowardly, meek, submissive, 198

    crabbiness, 154

    deception, 152

    deep hurt; longstanding resentment; deep secret or grief eating away at the self, 162

defeatism, 153
denying your own needs; not supporting yourself, 160, 199
depression, 51, 153, 155, 161, 166, 172, 173, 189, 193, 194
entitlement issues, 156
fear, 173
feeling attacked by life, 153
feeling defenseless / hopeless; nobody cares, 161
feeling like being caught between a rock and a hard place, 179
financial worries, 181
flexibility in attitudes, 180
flighty, 194
forgetful, 194
giving power/control to others, 159, 195
grief or suffocation, 169
holding onto old ideas, 174
inabilty to communicate, 195
inability to express one's self, 198
inability to express self love, 197
inability to learn, 193
inability to let go, 185
inadequate expression or acceptance of needs, 199
indeciveness, 173
internalize feelings, 179
irritable, 153, 160
    irritation to someone close to you, 166
humiliation, 155
jealousy/, 199
joyful, 168
lack of communication, 180
lack of concentration, 194
lack of joy flowing through life, 159
lack of self-confidance, 182
lack of strength, 182
lack of sweetness in life, 171

letting everyone's else needs come first, 199
loss of power, 182
love and people energy support, 180
needing to re-center on essentials of life, 183
negative thoughts, 196
not caring for oneself, 153
not feeling supported, 179
not speaking up, 179
obsession, 170, 171
overbearing attitudes, 184
overwhelmed, 181
passive aggressive, 194
possessive, 199
preoccupied, 194
rage, aggression control issues, 155
repressed feelings, fears, sexuality, 181
resentment, 168
restlessness, 149
running from life, 179
selfish, 152
self-worth issues, 75, 185, 194
sleep poorly, 153
strength, power, integrity, 183
support of basic needs, 181
survival issues, 155
sweetness in life, 171
tired all the time, 153
taking on too much responsibility, 180
unable to concentrate, 153
unable to ground into reality, 200
urealistic/overinflated view of self, 198
vulnerability, 196
wanting everything, 199
weak voice, 195
weight of the world on your shoulders, 179
worry, 171
empathy, 70, 108

emperor archetype. *See* king archetype
endocrine,
    glands, 152, 156
    system, 23, 37, 136, 155, **174**, 175
energetic body. *See* astral body
engineer archetype, 57
engrams, 34, 107, **188**
entities,35, 97, 100, 101, 104, **106**, 107, 121, 191
    block, 106
entrepreneur archetype. *See* pioneer archetype
environmental
    PRSM Chart body category, 37, 136
    descriptors, 135, **143**, 144
environmentalist archetype. *See* advocate archetype
ether element, 198
etheric
    body level, 103, 134, 137
    heart. *See* thymus chakra
    world intelligences, 22
excess of the bone, 167
exorcist archetype, 57
explorer archetype. *See* pioneer archetype
eyes, 37, 105, 135, **166**, 167, 172
    problems, 194
fairy godmother/godfather archetype. *See* angel archetype
fame/aspirations life area, 18
familial level of consciousness, 36
family/foundation life area, 17
father archetype, 58
fatigue, 154, 155, 159, 161, 200
fats, 144, 145, 155, 172
fear, 12, 18, 20, 40, 41, 68, 75, 83, 109, 119, 120, 154, 168, 175,
    179, 185, 189, 196, 199, 205, 207, 233,
    of water, 203
    repressed, 181
feeling unproductive, 152
feet, 174, **182**, 200
    burning/tingling, 161
    chronically cold, 200
    temperature swings, 200
feet / ankles / knees / hips, 182
femme fatale archetype, 42, 56, **58**
Feng Shui, 16, 17, 24, 100
fifth element. *See* ether
fight/flight response, 199
"find another spirit", 101
fingers, 184
fire element, 168, 175, 198
flame family, 35, 112, **139**
flirt archetype. *See* femme fatale archetype
floating feeling, 194
fluorine, 146
follower archetype. *See* student archetype
food
    groups, 125, 129, 140
    quality, 148
    sensitivities, 144
foot chakras, 24, 38, **200**
foot, leg, or lower body injuries, 200
forgiveness, 105
"forgiveness or apology needed", 93
free will, 31
fungus, 37, 135, **160**
galactic level of consciousness, 36
galactic time, 99
gallbladder, 37, 136, **172, 173**, 198
    and depression, 172
    and yeast infection, 160
    meridian, 167

gambler archetype, 59. *See also* addict archetype

gas, excessive, 161, 172

generational clearing, 7, 33

ghost, 96, 106, 121

gigolo archetype. *See* Don Juan archetype

glutton archetype. *See* addict archetype

god/goddess archetype, 41, **59**

golden shadow archetypes, 41

gonads, 37, 135, **152**, 156, 199

gossip archetype, 60

gourmet archetype. *See* hedonist archetype

greed, 152

grounding, 12, 78, 182, 199

difficulty, 200, 201

group consciousness, 97

growth and development, 156

guardian angels, 5, 13, 30, 31, 46, 96, 121, **134**, 145, 210

guide archetype, 60

guides, 5, 13, 30, 31, 67, 96, 121, **134**

guru archetype. *See* guide archetype

GV1, 199

GV20, 193

H8, 198

hand chakras, 23, 38, 136, **197**

hands/wrists/elbows/shoulders, 181, 197, 198

Hartmann Lines, 148

Hartmann Net, 148

hate, 168

head, 126, 179, 180, 193

diaphragms, 184

headaches, 149, 155, 172, 191

tension, 194

top or back of head, 193

healer archetype, 61, *See* knight archetype

healing grid, 5

health/unity life area, 17

hearing problems, 195

heart, 37, 56, 58, 135, 152, 153, **168**, 175, 180, 196

attack, 196

chakra, 13, 23, **196**, 197, 201, 207

constrictor, 175

vow, 94, 101, **105**, 107

heavy metals, 147

hedonist archetype, 62

helminths, 159

helpful people/travel life area, 17

hemorrhoids, 170, 199

herald archetype. *See* networker

hermit archetype, 62

hero/heroine archetype, 41, **63**

high heart chakra. *See* thymus chakra

high self, 13, 14, 18, **30**, 35, 96, 121, **134**, 138, 207, 208

Hippocrates, 118

hips, 180

homeless person archetype. *See* beggar

hormonal

body category, 37, 135

descriptors, 152

system, 191

house of the heart, 153

Huagai, 196

Huiyin, 199

human kingdom, 31

hunger and thirst control, 155

hydrocarbons, 147

hyper or hypothyroidism, 195

hypothalamus, 37, 135, 155, 156

I AM presence, 5, 7, 12, 22

iatrogenic, 37, 135, 147
Identifiers Chart, 140
immune system, 153, 158, 160, 161, 166, 170, 172, 173, 196, 197
imprints, 107
indigestion, 171
infection, **157**, 158, 161
    acute, 163
    bacterial, 159
    categories of, 37, 125, 135
    chronic, 163
    clinical levels, 162
    descriptors, 158
    gallbladder, 173
    hidden, 166
    localized, 163
    sinus, 161
    subacute, 163
    systemic, 163
    viral, 196
innocent child archetype. *See* magical child archetype
insomnia, 149, 166, 189
insulin, 156, 171, 189
    resistence, 209
integrate healing, 94
internal-meridial
    category, 37, **135**
    descriptors, 166
intestines, 156
intrusion, 104, 107
inventor archetype. *See* alchemist
Invocation, v, 5, **11**, 12, 13, 14, 207, 208
iodine, 146
irritable bowel syndrome, 199
itching, 144
jaw, 179
    problems, 126, 195
Jesus, 22

jing qi, 167, 173
joints, 181, 184
journalist archetype.*See* networker archetype
journey/career life area, 16
judge archetype, 63
Jung, Carl, 40, 134
K1, 200
karma, iii, 35, 93, 94, 95, 138, 199
Keywords, 6, 9, 44, 88, 94, 102, 110, 112, 113, 208, 209
    petals, 44, 92, **101, 102**
kidneys, 37, 136, 152, 154, 156, 160, 167, **173**, 174, 175, 183
    disease, 198
king archetype, 64
kingdoms. *See* three kingdoms
knees, 184, 199
knight archetype, 42, 64, 73, 75
knowledge/skills life area, 18
Krishna, 22
kundalini, 194
lactic acidosis, 161
large intestine, 37, 136, 169, 175
    and appendix, 169
    meridian, 167, 169
laryngitis, 195
larynx, 154
laterality, 180, 193
lazy kidneys, 154
Leadbeater, C.W., 107, 138
left-right brain synchronization. *See* laterality
legislator archetype. *See* advocate archetype
leg, 126, 174, 182, 200
    muscle spasms, 200
    pain, 172, 179
    tight /inflexible, 200
level of consciousness, 21, 78, 107
    Mayan, 29, **35, 36**

ley lines, 37, 135, **148**, 149
Lianquan, 196
liberator archetype, 65
life areas, 15, **16, 17**, 101
light energy, 96
limbic system, 155
lipodystrophy, 161
liver, 37, 135, 136, **153**, 156, 158,
    167, 170, **172**, 198
    and gallbladder, 173
    and thyroid, 155
lobbyist archetype. *See* advocate
    archetype
loose bowels, 154
lover archetype, 65
low back. *See* lumbar vertebra
Lowen, Alexander, 184
lower extremities, 199
lower mental-causal body, 137.
    See also emotional body level
lumbar vertebra, 101, 102, 180,
    181, 182, 199
lungs, 37, 136, 167, **169**, 175, 180,
    196
    and kidneys, 173
    meridian, 169
    rule skin, 185
lymph, 38, 136, 177, 184
    system, 151, 158, 170, **183**
lymphadenopathy, 161
lymphocytes, 153, 170
mad scientist archetype. *See* destroyer archetype
magician archetype. *See* alchemist
magnetic, 37, 135
malignant tumor, 162
mammalian level of consciousness, 36
mammary glands, 199
manager archetype. *See* Engineer
    archetype

martyr archetype, 66
master archetype. *See* teacher
    archetype, *See* mentor archetype
master gland, 156
matriarch archetype. *See* mother/
    maternal archetype
"*May I?*" "*Can I?*" "*Should I?*", 5
mediator archetype, 66. *See also*
    judge archetype
medical dowsing, 117, 118
menstrual problems, 199
mental body level, 6, 34, **35**, 104,
    112, 114, 120, 137, **138**, 139,
    157, 161, 162
mentally fatigued, 154
mentor archetype, 41, **67**
mercenary archetype. *See* warrior
    archetype
messenger archetype. *See* networker
messiah archetype, 67
metal element, 169
midas/miser archetype, 68
migraines, 194
milk production in pregnant
    women, 156
mineral balance, 153
minister archetype. *See* priest/
    priestess archetype
minstrel archetype. *See* storyteller
miracles, 51, 52, 94
modifiers, 125, 129, **140**
Mohammed, 22
monad. *See* mental body level
monk/nun archetype, 68
mother/maternal archetype, 40,
    69
mother nature archetype. *See*
    mother /maternal archetype
mouth, 195

mouth of the goddess. *See* alta
major chakra
multiple answers, 208
muscles, 19, 38, 136, 140, 168, 177, 183, **184**, 197, 198
pain and spasms, 200
tension, 104
musician archetype. *See* artist
Myss, Carolyn, 40
mystic archetype, 69
narrator archetype. *See* storyteller archetype
national level of consciousness, 36
natural laws, 94
nausea and vomiting, 161, 171, 188
neck, 153, 174, 179, **180**, 194, 195, 203
stiff, 193
negative emotions, 104
negative energy, 189
nerves, 19, 38, 130, 136, 140, 165, 168, 183, 184, **185**
optic, 194
thoracic inlet, 180
sciatic, 126, 132, 179, 181
nervous system, 155, 198, 199
central, 193
networker archetype, 70
neutral line, 6, 9, 19, 26, 33, 43, 88, 97, 104, 113, 114, 125, 126, 145, 146, 205, 208, 209
neutrality, 3, 4, 6, 26, 42, 43, 89, 101, 104, 114, 131, 210
neutral swing, 9, 26, 43, 113, 114, 125, 126, 145, 208, 209
nightmares, 194
nomad archetype. *See* seeker archetype
nonconformist archetype. *See* rebel archetype

nose, 167, 169
number chart, 10
nurse archetype. *See* healer archetype
nutritional PRSM section, 37, 135, **148**
obtain permission to work, 5
omega chakra, 23, 136, 192, **200**
openings, 101, 104, **106**
opposite of the problem, 93
optic nerve, 194
organic halogens, 146
organic solvents, 146
organs of elimination, 199
osteoporosis, 153
other's stuff, 94, 107
ovaries, 152, 156
oversoul, 139
pain, 13, 103, 149, 184, 185, 188, 207
abdominal, 160, 161
and scars, 185
as a disease signal, 117
back, 114, 120, 174
behind right shoulder blade, 161, 172
leg, 172, 179
lumbar, 101, 102, 199
muscle, 104
neck, 203
sacral, 132
sciatic, 126, 179, 181
temporary relief of, 120
tendon, 172
upper back, 197
pancreas, 37, 136, 156, 198
pancreatic duct, 168
paranoia, 154
parasites, 37, 135, **158**
classifications of, 158

parasympathetic nervous system, 195
parathyroid, 37, 135, 153, 195
  function, 153
parent archetype. *See* father archetype
past life, 33, 93, 99, 103, 124, 187, 188
  and ego, 134
  contract, 105
  deaths chart, 124, 203
  death memories, 204, 205
  time lock, 98
  patterns of dis-ease, 121
  relationships, 95, 97
  vow, 94
patriarch archetype. *See* father archetype
pelvis, 181, 184
pendulum
  drops off/moves to the left or right of neutral line, 145, 209
  source of information, 11, 29, **30**, 133, 134
Pendulum Research Sourcing Method Chart. *See* PRSM
perception blocks, 107, 108
perfectionist archetype, 42, 70
Personal Trinity, 6, 12, **30**, 88, 96, 97, 113, 114, 134, 135, 145, 205, 207, 208, 209
physical body level, iii, 6, 12, 13, 22, 30, **34**, 94, 100, 104, 107, 112, 117, 120, 121, 125, 128-130, 132, **136**, 137, 138, 144, 157, 162, 172, 188, 194, 207
pilgrim archetype. *See* pioneer archetype
pineal chakra. *See* brow chakra
pineal gland, **156**, 193, 194

pioneer archetype, 71
pirate archetype, 41, 71
pituitary, 37, 135, 155, **156**, 193
planetary level of consciousness, 36
Plato, 40
plotter archetype. *See* engineer archetype
pneumonia, 196
poet archetype. *See* artist archetype
power chakra. *See* solar plexus chakra
preacher archetype. *See* guide archetype
Preparedness Checklist, 6, 14
priest/priestess archetype, 72
prince archetype, 72
princess archetype, 73. *See also* damsel archetype
professor archetype. *See* teacher archetype
profiler archetype. *See* detective archetype
prolapsed organs, 170
prosperity life area, 17
prostate, 152
prostitute archetype, 73
protection, 12, 32, 58, 96, 189
protein, 153
protester archetype. *See* rebel archetype
protocols
  affirmation clearing, 26
  allergy testing, rapid, 145
  Basic LifeWeaving, **5-6**, 26, 33, 92, 93, 99, 101, 104, 114, 125, 130, 131, 145
  check that archetypes have cleared, 43

clearing cell memory of past life deaths, 205
completion check, 113
harmonize the *Personal Trinity*, 208
PRSM diagnosis, 125
therapeutic color exercise, 19
PRSM section B, 205
using the clearing macro, 112, 113
using the research chart, 88
protozoa, 158
PRSM chart, xv, 9, 37, 38, 88, 93, 115,118, 119, 123, 124,
diagnostic protocol, 125
example of working with, 126-132
modifiers, 139
Section B, deaths, 203-205
psychic attack, 38, 136, 187, 189
psychic weapon. *See* intrusion
psychoses, 193
puppet archetype. *See* slave archetype
qi, 168, 169, 185
queen archetype, 44, 74
quintessence. *See* ether
Rabbi archetype. *See* priest/priestess archetype
radiation, 37, 135, 148
radon gas, 148
rebel archetype, 74
recorder angels, 106
recreational drugs, 189
redeemer archetype. *See* messiah archetype
relationships, xv, 4, 33, 42, 88, 92, 139, 144, 169, 173, 185
and heart chakra, 196
and the elements, 19

block, 107
controlling, 195
life area, 16
PRSM section, 95
with self, 185
rescuer archetype. *See* knight archetype
Research Chart, xv, 6, 87, 88, **103**
resistance to healing, 94
respiratory system, 144
and thyroid, 154
responsible to/for, v, 15, **27**
revolutionary archetype. *See* rebel archetype
rheumatoid arthritis, 197
root chakra, 24, 191, **199**, 201
ruler archetype. *See* king archetype
saboteur archetype, 41, 75
Sacred Contracts, 40
sacred geometry, 22, 33
sacrum, 125, 129, 132, 181. *See also* coccyx, 199
sage archetype. *See* guide archetype
saints, 22, 102
samaritan archetype, 76
savior archetype. *See* messiah archetype, *See* avenger archetype
scars, 38, 136, 177, 185, 188
schemer archetype. *See* engineer archetype
scholar archetype, 41, 76
Schumann Waves/Resonance,148
sciatic nerve, 126, 132, 179, 181
scientist archetype. *See* alchemist
scribe archetype, 77
sculptor archetype. *See* artist archetype
sea of food and fluid, 171

sea of marrow, 166
seat of our ego, 171
seat of the soul, 196
seat of self-identity, 198
secretary archetype. *See* scribe archetype
seducer archetype. *See* Don Juan archetype
seductress archetype. *See* femme fatale archetype
seeker archetype, **77**
seizure, 194
self, 12, **13**, 20, **30**, 95, 96, 112-114, 134, 162, 192, 198, 207
   divine, 22
   shadow, 40, 41
self, soul and ego. *See Personal Trinity*
self-respect, a need for, 81
Selye, Hans, 144
sense of purpose, loss of, 194
separates, **96**, 97, 106
seraph, 96
serial killer archetype. *See* destroyer archetype
servant archetype, 78
settler archetype. *See* pioneer archetype
sex addict archetype. *See* Don Juan archetype
sex hormones, 153
sexual chakra. *See* abdominal chakra
sexual function, 155
sexual organs. *See* gonads
shadow archetypes, **40, 41**, 42, 44-83
shaman archetype. *See* priest/priestess archetype, *See* exorcist archetype
Shanzong, 197

Shaofu, 198
shapeshifter archetype, 78
Shen, 168
Shimen, 199
shoulders, **181**, 184, 161, 172, 179
sinus, 37, 135, 161, **166**
   and yeast infection, 160
   sinusitis, 172, 194
siren archetype. *See* femme fatale archetype
skeletal system, 195 199,
skin, **185**, 198
   and cells, 38, **185**, 136
   pigmentation, 156
   rashes, 144
skull, 166, 179, 194. *See also* cranium
slave archetype, 41, **79**
sleep and awake states, 155
sludge, 37, 135, **160**, 161, 173
small intestine, 37, 135, 136, **168**, 169, 175
sneezing, 144
solar plexus, 184
   chakra, 23, **198**, 201
soul, 13, **30**, 31, 35, 93, 96, 106, 107, 120, 138, 188, 192, 201, 208
   assigned, 31, 134
   chakra, 23, **192**, 136
   committee, 5, 13, 14, 18, 96, 134, 207
   family, 35, **139**
   mate, 112, 139
   mind, 20, 22, 117, 118, 137, 138, 139
   programs,101, 104, 105, **107**
   seat of the, 196
   twin, 35, 96, 139
soul star chakra. *See* soul chakra
sound frequencies, 4

Source, vi, vii, 5, 12, 22, 28, **31**, 35, 96, 97, 134, 139

source of information, pendulum, 29, **30**, 31, 133, 134

poor, 134

spell block, 106

spine, 23, 152, 166, 173, 180, 181, 192, 199, 200

and chakras, 191

spirit gateways. *See* openings

spirit guides, 5, 13, 30, 31, **96**, 121, 134, 145, 210

archetype, **60**, 67

spirit helpers, 6, 7, 101, 106, 114, **134**, 145, 209

upgrading, 13

spiritual body level, 6, **35**, 100, 104, 112, 114, 120, 121, 130, **139**

spiritual master archetype. *See* guide archetype

spiritual nanny, 13, 30

Spiritual Response Therapy, xiii

spleen, 37, 136, **170**, 171, 199

chakra. *See* abdominal chakra

spoiler archetype. *See* destroyer archetype

spy archetype. *See* detective archetype

St. Germaine, 22

stability, grounding, balance, 182

Standard Process Laboratories, 154

star energy, 20

stiffness, 184

stomach, 37, 136, 168, **171**, 198

meridian, 167

ulcers, 198

stones or sludge, 37, 135, 160

"*stop for now*", 95

storyteller archetype, 79

stress, 25, 37, 135, 144, 169, 188, 191, 200

stroke, 194, 196

structural, 38, 126, 166, 168, 169, 172, 173

modifiers, 129

descriptors, 140, **179**

identifiers, 125, **182-183**

PRSM category, 127, 129, 131, 132, 136, **177**, 182

student archetype, 80

subconscious mind, 17, 25, 30, 40, 42-44, 104, 112, 119, 121, 134, 159, 187, 191

superconscious mind, 119, 187

Supplemental Questions, 6

swindler archetype. *See* thief archetype

switchboard of the body, 166

T-1, 154

T-3, 154

T-4, 155

T-4 1/2, 155

tailbone. *See* sacrum

taiyin, 200

teacher archetype, 80

teeth, 37, 135, **166**, 167, 179, 199

temporal-mandibular joint.*See* jaw

tendons, 172, **184**

"*test age.*", 33

testes, 152

thalamus, 155

The Complete System of Self-Healing Internal Exercises, 151

the One. *See* Source

therapist archetype. *See* healer archetype

thief archetype, 81

third ear. *See* crown chakra

third eye. *See* brow chakra

thoracic inlet nerve plexus, 180
  diaphragm, 184
thoracic nerve, 180, 184
thoracic vertebrae, 180
thought body. *See* mental body
  level
thought forms, 32, **107**, 189, 191
three kingdoms, 29, **31**, 37, 102,
  135
throat, 37, 135, 154, **166**, 167,
  195, 196
  chakra, 23, **195**, 201
  sore, 195
thrush, 161
thymus, 37, 135, **153**, 175, 196
  chakra, 23, **196**, 201
thyroid, 37, 135, 140, 153, **154,
  155**, 156, 175, 180, 195
  sub-categories, 154, 155
thyroxin. See T-4
time, Research Chart category, 29,
  33, 92, **97-98**
timeline clearing, 98
T-lymphocytes, 153
tongue, 168
tonsillitis, 195
toxic metals, 147
toxic streams, 37, 135, 148, 149
toxins, 37, 135, 157, 158, 173
trachea, 196
trauma, 104, 121, 166
  block, 107
  childhood, 187, 188
treatment approach choices, 120,
  140
tribal level of consciousness, 36
trickster archetype, 81
triiodothyronine. *See* T-3
triple burner meridian, 167, 175
triple warmer meridian. *See* triple
  burner

tumor, 162, 194
tunnel vision, 119
tutor archetype. *See* mentor
  archetype
unconditional love, 4, 7, 40, 89,
  105, 113, 168
underground streams, 143
universal level of consciousness,
  36
urge to smoke, 195
urinary bladder, 37, 136, **174**, 175,
  199
uterus, 152, 199
vagina, 152
vampire archetype, 82
Versandaal, D.A., 154
victim archetype, 41, 82
Violet Flame, iii, v, 5, 7, 12, 21, 22
virgin archetype, 83
virus, 37, 135, 157, 159, 161,
visionary archetype. *See* dreamer
  archetype
visual clarity, 193
vows, 97, 104, **105**, 107, 204
  heart, 94, 101, 105, 107
  hidden, 94, 101, 105, 107
  past life, 94
wanderer archetype. *See* seeker
  archetype
warrior archetype, 41, 83. *See also*
  knight archetype
water
  element, **20**, 21, 35, 137,
  174, 175, 196, 199
  elementals, 32
  metabolism, 156
  retention, 154
weaver archetype. *See* artist archetype
wei chi, 180, 189
weight issues, 199, 203

gain, 159
inability to lose, 159
loss, 161
White Light
column, 5, 12
tunnel, 5, 7
wise woman archetype. *See* guide
archetype
wizard archetype. *See* alchemist
wood element, 172, 173
word frequencies, 4, 101

word petals. *See* Keyword petals
workaholic archetype. *See* addict
archetype
worksheet, LifeWeaving, 5, 14,
212
world chaos block, 108
wounded healer, 61
yeast, 37, 135, 157, 160, 199
Yintang, 194
Zhongwen, 198

About the Author

Carole Conlon, M.T. (ASCP), L.Ac., holds the NCCAOM national board certification as Diplomate of Acupuncture. Following a 1984 graduation from the Northwest Institute of Acupuncture and Oriental Medicine in Seattle, Washington, and an internship at the Chongqing Institute of Traditional Chinese Medicine in Chongqing, China, Carole worked as an acupuncturist in Washington State for 21 years. During that time she specialized in Nogier's Auriculomedicine method.

Prior to her acupuncture studies, Carole worked as a registered medical technologist in a variety of hospital settings for 12 years, including serving five years in Barrow and Bethel Alaska Indian Health Service Hospitals. She earned a Master's degree in Management and Supervision in the Health Care Field through Central Michigan University during those years.

During the time Carole practiced traditional acupuncture, she also began developing a pendulum testing and healing method called LifeWeaving. Then in 2006, a paradigm-shifting course clarified her life destiny and in order to better embrace that mission, Carole began to upgrade and transform both herself and the pendulum method and started working more on an energetic, emotional and spiritual approach with patients.

Through LifeWeaving, Carole is able to re-code and re-calibrate a person's mental and emotional bodies in order to reverse and eliminate patterns of fear, karma, limitation, and self-sabotage. This method results in increased harmony, freedom from suffering and a marvelous synchronicity with all aspects of life and eases the transition into the coming Golden Age.

Now residing in New Mexico, Carole uses auricular acupuncture, nutritional counseling, LifeWeaving clearing, teaching and writing to help clients improve their own core health and wellbeing by restoring their ayni - their sacred relationship - with themselves, with each other, with the environment, with their own health, and even with existence itself.

On a personal note, Carole enjoys the abundant sunshine of New Mexico and very much likes dragons.

Great Ayni!

Books and charts are available at www.AyniLifeWeaving.com and Amazon.com. For up-to-date information, changes and tips for the LifeWeaving system, visit www.AyniLifeWeaving.com.

42153859R00141

Made in the USA
Middletown, DE
11 April 2019